HASHGACHAH
PRATIS
השגחה פרטית

HASHGACHAH PRATIS
השגחה פרטית

An Exploration of
Divine Providence and Free Will
על עומק דרכי ההשגחה
והבחירה החופשית

RABBI ARYEH LEIBOWITZ

First Edition 2009
Revised Edition 2012
Softcover Edition 2014
Copyright © 2009 by Aryeh Leibowitz
ISBN-13: 978-1477660720

First Edition Published by:
TARGUM PRESS, INC.

The author can be contacted by email at Ajleibow@gmail.com

Rabbi Zev Leff

Rabbi of Moshav Matityahu
Rosh HaYeshiva—Yeshiva Gedola Matityahu

הרב זאב לף בס״ד

מרא דאתרא מושב מתתיהו
ראש הישיבה—ישיבה גדולה מתתיהו

D.N. Modiin 71917   טל׳ Tel: 08—976—1138   Fax: 08—976—5326 ׳פקס   ד.נ. מודיעין 71917

Dear Friends,

I have read the manuscript of "Hashgacha Pratis" by Aryeh Leibowitz and have found it extremely informative. The author presents a very in depth study of the various perspectives of Divine providence as found in the classic Jewish sources.

In true Talmudic fashion he presents, analyzes and resolves the various questions on each perspective. He further develops a consistent theme through which he admirably harmonizes the various apparently conflicting views into a homogeneous perspective on the topic.

The style of the presentation will be familiar to a Talmudic student, but it is presented in a manner than can be understood by all. It is not light reading, but studying it will be informative and enjoyable.

I highly recommend it as a source for understanding this important and often misunderstood topic. The more we understand G-d's consciousness of us we become more and more conscious of G-d.

May Hashem grant the author and his family long life and health to continue to merit the community with further Torah works.

Sincerely,
With Torah blessings

Rabbi Zev Leff

Rabbi Hershel Schachter
94 Bennett Avenue
New York, New York 10033
(212) 795-0630

הרב צבי שכטר
ראש ישיבה ורב כולל
ישיבת רבינו יצחק אלחנן

מתנת דברי

יפה כח, יקרי, ידידי הרב...

כתב /התחא... הרב וכו'...

שמת באלגיות על...ל הסתרת...

שרבני מארכא מקהלת – ... ...

כ/...תניות, ענין ..., ודיני בחירת ...

...ד ... וברוכה ... ...

...שמר/ ... את ...

...ה ... התורה והיו...

...ע ושלום.

הכותב ו... לכבוד ולענין התורה

צבי שכטר

תשו"ג.

מוסדות עופל בת-ציון

ישיבת "אהלי יעקב"

מתיבתא "יוסף חיים ושלום"

כולל "נתיבות עולם"

נוסד שנת תשמ"ה

ע"י ורה"ג ר' מאיר בעלסקי שליט"א

מס' עמותה 58-011-133-4

מס' בארה"ב 36-3566181

רח' אלפנדרי 32 ירושלים עה"ק תובב"א סל. 02-5381949

הרב דניאל בעלסקי, מנהל

בס"ד

ערי"ח סיון תשס"ז

ירושלים עה"ק תו'

יום ס"ד למספר בנ"י

לכבוד ש"ב רחימא ונפשאי אב-רך הטופל בכל מדה נכונה

הר"ר אריה יעקב נ"י

אמרו חז"ל על המעמד של כניסה לברית, מברך מה הוא אומר. אין ספק שיש מברך. השאלה היא רק על נוסח הברכה. וכן בדיין. הדואה מברך, הדואה פרי עמל של נפש יקרה נקי הדעת וטהור הלב מברך. מברך לנתן התורה שעשה יום זה. ומברך הבוחר בחכמים ובמשנתם. זכית לשנים. זכית לחדוש ולחזור פיריות יפות בשדה נטושה, מחד גיסא, ובעידית שבעידית מתורתינו הקדושה מאידך גיסא. בא תחבקוק והזקמידין על אחת, ובאחת תמכת יסודותיך. אשריך ואשרי יולדתך. שנים על שנים אנו עומדים מסתאים על הברכה השרוייה בכל מעשי ידיך ומצפים לראות בגאולת כחות נפשך הווהדית והנה הגיע הזמן לברך על המוגמר, ראשית פרי אדמתך.

הקב"ה נתן לך לשון לימודים. לך בכחך זה ועלה רס, מורשת אבותינו הקדושים אשר בארץ. כאשר זכית לסדר אותה, מצוה גדולה זו, כן תזכה לעשותה. ומי יתן ויהיו דברי היקר"ים הגעינים מתקבלים בי מדרשא, עלים על שלחן מלכים (מאן מלכי רבנן) ועושים חיל בבית לחם, לחמה של תורה.

הכורי"ח לכבודה של תורה וקוסקיה

הרב דניאל בעלסקי

בן אמריר הגרי"ם שליט"א

חתן מריח הגרי"ג בולמן זצ"ל

CONTENTS

PREFACE

Most people associate *hashgachah pratis*, divine providence, with incredible life-altering stories of overt
divine intervention. And indeed, bookstores are already filled with inspiring collections of this nature.
However, many individuals fail to see *hashagachah pratis* as a daily
force in even the most mundane situations.

Moreover, most people also do not realize that differing views of
hashgachah pratis are found in the literature of Jewish thinkers. They
may stumble across a rabbinic source and, due to their unfamiliar-
ity with the terms and concepts, emerge with a misunderstanding
of the true intent of the author. They claim that the Rambam holds
this way, or the *Ohr ha-Chayim* that way, for they have not seen the
entire context, nor are they aware of the philosophic framework in
which these opinions were expressed.

The goal of this work is to address both of the above mentioned
issues. In these pages, an attempt is made to demonstrate the extent
of *hashgachah pratis* in daily life, by providing a rigorous and thor-

ough analysis of the various Jewish perspectives on divine providence. Jewish thought, like all other disciplines in Jewish scholarship, is highly sophisticated, and cannot be captured in a single lined mantra. By developing the various schools of thought in Jewish tradition, as well as suggesting perspectives to harmonize the differing views, this book seeks to provide a sophisticated approach to viewing God's involvement in our personal lives.

To this end, primary sources occupy a central position in this work. Many of these sources appear for the first time ever in English translation. The purpose is to allow the sources to speak for themselves, and to invite the reader to confront the Jewish thinkers in their own words. Certainly the analysis of the sources is open to discussion, and the understandings presented in this work are not always the only way to read the sources. The reader is encouraged to consult the original Hebrew, and turn this book into an active learning experience, in place of a passive reading experience.

One last point is in order. No book, and certainly not by this author, can truly explain how God's providence works. God's designs are beyond human comprehension. In a sense this work is itself a paradox, as it attempts to classify and explain something which ultimately defies classification and explanation. The reader is forewarned that the principles learned are only general, and that this discussion is not the final word, but rather just the beginning.

The purpose of this work is to clarify and resolve vexing issues related to divine providence, yet for every issue it resolves, many new questions are raised. Ultimately, the goal is to evoke serious thought and contemplation on the issues surrounding divine providence. It is my sincere hope that with God's help this work increases your consciousness of God.

ACKNOWLEDGMENTS

The work for this book spanned formative years of my life, and I was privileged to have various forms of assistance as the work developed.

I am indebted to Rabbi Daniel Belsky and Rabbi Chaim Dovid Saperstein for the time they spent discussing many of the issues in this book with me. Additionally, the following people contributed in different ways, be it through engaging me in discussions, late-night calls with a recently discovered source, or overall encouragement to see this work through to completion: Rabbi Mayer Twersky, Rabbi Ari Waxman, Rabbi Moshe Jacobowitz, Rabbi David Kahn, Rabbi Netanel Lauer, Rabbi Shmuel Maybruch, and Daniel Nagel.

Certain works were also valuable in my research, and I wish to acknowledge Rabbi Chayim Friedlander's *Sifsei Chayim*, Rabbi Dov Halperin's *Chemda Genuza*, and Rabbi Nahum Spirn's *Why Me?*

While completing this book, divine providence provided me the merit of finding my life partner, Chana. Chana's dignified personality and her passionate devotion to *middos* and Torah-true values serve as an example for my own growth. For these reasons, and many others, she is the backbone of our family.

In the years between completion of this book and publication, my wife and I have been blessed with two wonderful children, Tehila and Malka Elisheva. We are thankful to Hashem for the opportunity and challenge to raise them in the ways of His Torah, and pray that we merit to see much *nachas* from them.

My parents, Dr. Martin and Rhonda Leibowitz, have always served as role models and have taught me how to live as a thinking, religious member of society. Their constant support and encouragement for every project in my life has been a driving force behind all that I do, and I can never thank them enough. My parents are also the first readers of everything I write, always offering valuable comments and insights. I especially thank my father for his assistance with the editing of this book. I also wish to acknowledge my dear siblings, Sammy and Ronit, Yoni, Benjy, and Shoshana.

My in-laws, Rabbi Baruch and Paula Chait, have encouraged me with everything I have set my heart to. I thank them, and the entire extended Chait family, for their love and support.

I would also like to take this opportunity to mention my paternal grandparents, Baba and Grandpa Weiser, and my maternal grandmother, Nanny Perchick, who have always showered me with their love and are very dear to my heart. My maternal grandfather, Dada Perchick, *a"h*, was *niftar* when I was a young teenager, but his dedication to honesty and integrity and his loving concern for my development will remain with me forever. Although I never met him, the memory of my father's father, Aryeh Leib ben Sender Asher, *a"h*, continues to this day as his values, humor, and interests contribute greatly to our family.

The entire staff of Targum Press also deserve thanks for making this project into what it is today. Although I never had a chance to meet him, the knowledge of R. Dombey's, *z"l*, interest and support for a different kind of work by an unknown writer served as a source of encouragement through the long process of publication.

The foresight, sensibility, and wisdom of my editor, Ita Olesker, is responsible for the professionalism found within these pages, and her own sensitivities and values contributed greatly to this work.

All endeavors in life only reach fruition through the guiding attention of the Almighty. I thank Hashem for all He has given me and for providing me the opportunity to publish this work. It is my fervent prayer that the ideas contained within are pleasing in His eyes, and only serve to increase *kavod Shamayim* in the world.

INTRODUCTION

Belief in a Creator is a foregone conclusion for many individuals seeking the truth. However, after such an affirmation, the individual craving divine knowledge confronts an unknown. To what extent, if any at all, does God interact with the world He created?

Jewish thought champions the belief in *hashgachah*, divine providence. In other words, Torah Judaism maintains that God cares about, and is actively involved in, what transpires under the cosmos.

Rabbi Moshe ben Nachman,[1] the Ramban, notes that the concept of divine providence entails two separate, distinct convictions.

We must believe that God knows all individual creatures and the details of their lives. [This knowledge includes] the heavenly creatures and the sublunary creatures, their actions and thoughts, and the past, present, and future...

After [proclaiming belief in divine knowledge] we affirm

---

1. Spain, d. 1270.

belief in divine governance and guardianship. We declare and affirm that which the verse states, "Great in counsel and un-fathomable in action, Your eyes are fixed upon all the ways of mankind..." (Jeremiah 32:19).[2]

Here we see that a belief in divine providence implies that 1) God has an intimate knowledge of everything that occurs in the universe, and 2) God governs the affairs of mankind. Affirmation of both divine knowledge and divine governance constitutes belief in divine providence.

Certainly, denial of God's knowledge constitutes a heretical re-jection of His divinity. However, perhaps a denial of God's gover-nance is not necessarily as theologically abominable. Considering God's immeasurable greatness, one may question His involvement in our lowly world. Why would God bother, or defile, Himself with the doings of our insignificant existence?[3] In a sense, man can con-ceivably reject the concept of God's governance due to a sincere, yet misguided, perception of His grandeur.[4]

Jewish thought utterly rejects this perspective. In the Hallel prayer, the verse from Psalms 113 declares, "Who is like our God, who sits upon high, yet lowers Himself to observe the heavens and the earth." Unlike those who argue that God's greatness precludes Him from governing the lowly world, the Psalmist tells us that God's greatness is specifically manifest in the fact that He can lower Himself to gov-ern the lowly world without diminution from His grandeur.[5]

---

2. Introduction to Ramban's commentary on Job.

3. In fact, this very argument is utilized by many Jewish thinkers to explain why God's governance does not extend to animals and plants.

4. This perspective may stem from a sincere outlook on God's grandeur, but its ramifications are catastrophic. Rabbi Yisrael Meir ha-Kohen Kagan (Poupko), the Chafetz Chayim (Poland, d. 1933), in his work *Shem Olam*, suggests that denial of divine providence based on misappropriated "respect" for God's grandeur was the catalyst for the emergence of idolatry in the generation of Enosh.

5. Rabbi Moshe Chayim Luzzato's *Mesillas Yesharim*, chapter 25:

This perspective is reiterated later in Psalms 138, "For God is exalted, yet He observes the lowly." The *Metzudas David* commentary[6] expounds:

> Even though He is very exalted, He observes the lowly and governs him to sustain him. Even though His dwelling place is in the heights of the heavens, He nevertheless chastises sinners from a distance.

A Long History of Denial

The denial of divine providence has a long history. The Ramban, in his Torah commentary (Exodus 13:16), states that already in the days of Enosh, people began to deny divine providence.

> From the time that idolatry appeared in the world in the days of Enosh, religious faith began to be confounded. Some rejected [God] completely, saying that the world is eternal [and was never created]. They denied God and said He is not [existent]. And there were some who denied His knowledge of particulars, and said: "How can God know? Is there knowledge above?" (Psalms 73:11). And there were also those who admitted to God's knowledge, but denied divine providence, thus equating man with the fish of the sea — who are not governed [with divine providence], and have no system of reward and punishment. Such people say, "God has forsaken the world" (Ezekiel 8:12).[7]

The way to acquire fear and awe of God is to meditate upon two realities... God governs over every small and great thing. Nothing is hidden from His eyes on account of it being too great or too lowly. For, in fact, every great thing as well as every lowly thing, both the despised and the respected, God sees and considers. He makes no distinction.

6. Commentary of Rabbi David Altschuler (Prague, d. 17th century) and his son Rabbi Hillel (Prague, d. 18th century).

7. Note that this approach of the Ramban is different from the view of the Chafetz Chayim quoted in a footnote above. The Ramban suggests that widespread denial of divine providence was a result of the proliferation of idolatry. The Chafetz Chayim says the opposite — that the proliferation of

Other episodes in Jewish history also feature denial of divine providence. In the book of Ezekiel (8:12), an angel seeking to demonstrate to Ezekiel the proliferation of idolatry in the land, quotes the sacrilegious rationalization of the idolaters: "God does not see us, God has forsaken the world." Rabbi David Kimchi,[8] the Radak, comments:

> They said, "God has forsaken the world." In other words, He doesn't govern in the lower world, rather only in the heavens, which [is the domain of] the heavenly spheres and the angels.[9] However, regarding the issues of this world, He doesn't govern at all, for He has left it to man, and they may do what they please. This is similar to what the evil people say, "Clouds hide [God], and He does not see, and so He walks around in the celestial sphere" (Job 22:14).

But denial of divine providence does not always stem from a mistaken perspective of God's grandeur. Emotional factors could undoubtedly contribute to an individual's rejection of divine providence. Our world has been the stage of much suffering, cruelty, and evil that continue to plague mankind. These vexing realities have led many to question the presence of an attentive God in history. Confronted with the ever-presence of evil, some may conclude that God couldn't possibly still care about the world He created. Could a benevolent God truly orchestrate the atrocities visited upon man-

---

idolatry was a result of the widespread denial of divine providence.

8. France, d. 1235.

9. In *Shem Olam*, part 1, chapter 3, the Chafetz Chayim dismisses this approach and cogently argues that compared to the exalted intangible greatness of God, even the angels and other heavenly hosts are completely insignificant, and that the logic that precludes God's governance over humanity would equally apply to the angelic creations. The Chafetz Chayim further suggests that this is the true intent of the above quoted verse from Psalms, "Who is like our God, who sits upon high, yet lowers Himself to observe the heavens and the earth." The implication of the verse is that it is also an act of "lowering" by God when He observes the heavens, just as when He observes the earth.

kind? Deniers reason that tragedy and travesty point towards a disorderly existence, a world bereft of a divine director.

Psychological factors could also account for the challenge of belief in divine providence. God's ways are beyond human comprehension. For this reason, man is often forced to understand God in human terms, despite the fact that these terms will always fall short of capturing the true essence of God and His actions. The Torah will often resort to anthropomorphic and anthropopathic terminology when retelling God's actions. For instance, God does not truly have eyes, in a physical sense; however, in order for we humans to have any conception of an act of "seeing" by God, the Torah speaks of His "eyes." The same is true regarding emotions and attributes. We say God acts with righteousness, fully aware that the human, this-worldly term "righteousness" will never completely explain God's righteousness. We hope that human acts of righteousness are similar enough to God's acts of "righteousness" that we will emerge with some understanding of this aspect of God's interaction with the world.

This helpful technique, however, can also pervert reality, and therefore must be carefully scrutinized. When pondering divine providence, man may mistakenly equate human governance with divine governance. When man creates an object, or invests time in a project, doesn't he quickly lose interest in his handiwork? How long does one invest continual effort in a project after it has been completed? Even if he does devote an hour or two, here and there, to a completed project, it never continues to be his sole investment. It is inconceivable to the human mind that one would create something, and then devote uninterrupted time to the preservation of this creation.

Yet, Isaiah's words ring clear, "For My thoughts are not like your thoughts" (Isaiah 55:8). God does not operate in the same way as man does, and God's governance of His created world, even long after He created it, continues unabated forever and ever.

A Major Foundation of Jewish Thought

The belief in divine providence occupies a central position in the world of Jewish thought. Rabbi Moshe ben Maimon,[10] the Rambam, in his introduction to *Perek Chelek*, delineates thirteen principles of Jewish dogma, known as the Thirteen Principles of Faith. The Rambam contends that these principles are so basic to Judaism that one who fails to internalize them has no share in the World to Come.

The tenth principle reads:

God knows the actions of man and never ceases to observe them [lit. to raise His eye from them]. Not like those who say, "God has forsaken the land" (Ezekiel 8:12), but rather like the verses read: "Great in counsel and unfathomable in action, Your eyes are fixed upon all the ways of mankind" (Jeremiah 32:19). "And God saw that the wickedness of man had increased throughout the land" (Genesis 6:5). And the verse also reads, "The cry of Sodom and Gomorrah has become great" (Genesis 18:20). These verses demonstrate the tenth principle.

The Rambam states that one must believe that God has knowledge of human activity and that He "never ceases to observe them." This second clause, "never ceases to observe them," may be a reference to divine governance. If so, the tenth principle contains both elements delineated in the beginning of this introduction that constitute belief in divine providence — divine knowledge and divine governance.

Support for this suggestion is forthcoming upon cross-referencing the verses quoted.[11] By demonstrating that the Rambam quot-

---

10. Spain-Egypt, d. 1204.

11. The Rambam's presentation of this principle is unique in that almost his entire text is quotations of biblical verses. This format yields a clouded view of the Rambam's true intent. We should note that the thirteen principles of the Rambam were abridged, not by the Rambam himself, and were appended to the end of the morning prayer service. Interestingly, the tenth

ed some of these verses not as references to divine knowledge, but as references to divine governance, we can cogently argue that the Rambam's intention in the tenth principle was also to mandate belief in divine providence.

The first verse referenced is from Ezekiel 8:12, "God has forsaken the land." In his *Moreh Nevuchim* (*Guide to the Perplexed*), the Rambam quotes this verse and directly relates it to those who deny divine providence. In section 3, chapter 17, the Rambam discusses the opinion of Aristotle that most things occur as a product of chance and happenstance. The Rambam argues emphatically that this view is incorrect, and he concludes:

> Those who believe in this view... are those who declare, "God has forsaken the land" (Ezekiel 8:12).[12]

The verses from Genesis 6:5 and 18:20 are also understood by the Rambam in other contexts as referring to God's active involvement in the world, and not merely to His knowledge of events. In *Hilchos Teshuvah* (3:2), the Rambam writes:

> An individual whose transgressions outnumber his merits dies immediately in his state of wickedness, as the verse reads, "On account of your many sins" (Jeremiah 30:14). So too, a country whose transgressions outnumber [their merits] is destroyed immediately, as the verse reads, "The cry of Sodom and Gomorrah has become great" (Genesis 18:20). And so too, the entire world - if their transgressions outnumber [their merits], it is destroyed immediately, as the verse reads, "And God saw that the wickedness of man had increased throughout the land" (Genesis 6:5).

In addition to the indications found in the above verses, our

---

principle is the only one that contains a biblical quotation as support for the principle. It is true that the actual wording of the abridged version indicates that the author did not think providence was included in the tenth principle. But, there are other instances in the abridged version where the stress is seemingly different than that of the Rambam.

12. In *Moreh Nevuchim* 3:54 the Rambam again clearly applies this verse to those who reject divine providence.

argument is supported by analyses of many Jewish thinkers. Rabbi Yosef Albo,[13] in his *Sefer ha-Ikarim* (1:15), states more than once that the Rambam indeed included divine providence in his tenth principle.

> If one counts divine knowledge and divine providence as one principle of faith, as the Rambam includes them in one principle of faith, then...[14]

This assumption regarding the inclusion of divine providence is also made by Rabbi Moshe Alshich[15] when he references the Rambam's principles.[16]

> Divine providence [is one of the principles], for He knows the actions of man and never ceases to observe them, as they say, "God has forsaken the land" (Ezekiel 8:12).

Whether divine providence is included in the Rambam's thirteen principles may be debated, but its centrality to Jewish thought is undeniable. As noted in the beginning of this introduction, the Ramban champions the belief in divine providence in his commentary on Job. Not only does he state that belief in divine providence is a major foundation in Jewish thought, but he also castigates one who fails to internalize such a belief, condemning him to losing his share in the World to Come.

> It is clear and well known that belief in divine knowledge...and [belief] in His providence, on a general and specific level, are major foundations of the Torah of Moses. For one who denies and says that God does not know the individual lowly creatures

---

13. Spain, d. 1444.

14. A few paragraphs later Rabbi Albo again states that divine providence is included in the tenth principle.

15. Israel, d. 1593.

16. *Sefer Toras Moshe, Devarim* 5:3. The Chafetz Chayim in *Shem Olam* 1:3 also takes it as a given that divine providence is included in the Rambam's thirteen principles. However he does not specifically mention a reference to the tenth principle.

and their doings, denies the entire Torah. Similarly, one who denies divine providence, saying that God does not govern man, [and that God does not care if] man does good or evil, [or] if they experience profit and success or pain and mishap — [for] all is chance to them — [such an individual] is undesirable by God, and God does not concentrate on him. Moreover, such a person has no portion in the World to Come.[17]

This attitude, assigning the belief in divine providence a vital role in Jewish thought, is further echoed by many later thinkers. For example, read the following declaration by Rabbi Yitzchak Abuhav[18] in his *Menoras ha-Meor* (292):

All the foundations of the Torah and faith are built upon belief in complete divine providence: how there is constant [governance] by God over the generalities and specifics, and how He provides for all based on their actions.[19]

With the recognition that divine providence is a major foun-

---

17. The Ramban in his essay *Toras Hashem Temimah* lists what he believes to be the three major foundations of Judaism. One of these is belief in divine providence, accompanied by belief in creation ex nihilo, and belief in divine knowledge. See Maharal's *Gevuros Hashem*, chapter 47, for a beautiful exposition of these three principles based on the biblical narrative of the splitting of the sea.

18. Spain, d. 14th century. Not to be confused with the other Rabbi Yitzchak Abuhav, Rabbi of Castile, Spain, who died in 1493 and wrote a super-commentary on the Ramban's Torah commentary.

19. Note also that in *Orchos Chayim* (#26), attributed to Rabbi Asher ben Yechiel (Rosh), we even find that a full belief in God's unity is contingent upon an internalized realization of divine providence. Expounding the verse in Deuteronomy 5:6, "I am Hashem, your God, that brought you out of the land of Egypt...," the *Orchos Chayim* writes:

    For one who does not believe that God "brought you out of the land of Egypt" [cannot truly] believe that "I am the Lord, your God." [This person therefore] lacks a complete belief in God's unity, [for the belief in divine providence] is the characteristic that the Jews have over and above the other nations of the world, and it is the foundation of the entire Torah.

dation of Jewish thought, the thinking religious individual must examine it in more detail, exploring its manifestations and defining its limitations.

To Strengthen Our Belief

One last discussion is appropriate before we confront the intricacies of divine providence. It has been argued that there are two types of truths. *Objective truths* are bits of knowledge and information that can be proven empirically. One plus one equals two is an example of an objective truth. *Subjective truths* are values, morals, things that one believes in his heart. The positive values of compassion, sensitivity, and justice are examples of subjective truths.

When something is part of the very fabric of one's existence, it is a subjective truth. These truths are not proven, nor are they easily communicated. They are felt. They are experienced. They are talked around, talked about, but not explainable. A rebel fighter who gives his life for a cause does so because deep in his heart he knows his cause to be true. He can't necessarily prove the truth of his cause, yet he knows that it is part of his existence and a vital component of his perceived reality.

Subjective truths often guide our daily lives. When one sees a destitute soul begging on the street for spare change, it is usually not an intellectual calculation that leads him to assist the poor individual. Rather one's generosity is evoked by an internalized moral sense of compassion, an internalized belief in the value and importance of altruism. The immediate sense of compassion stirred when the beggar extends his hand is the workings of a subjective truth.

A similar distinction is found in the writings of Jewish thinkers. *Chochmah* is information culled from one's study and experiences. It is empirical data, provable and explainable. It is information you simply know. *Da'as* is knowledge that cannot be proven empirically. It is information that has been internalized and affects the way one lives. It is information that has become a part of one's essence, such as the belief that happiness is achieved through fulfilling one's potential.

Chochmah does not have to affect the way one conducts his life, but *da'as* always will. *Da'as* is knowledge that one lives by. Morals, virtues, and other existential truths compose one's *da'as*.

Often something is learned as pure information — as *chochmah* — and over time is internalized and enters the realm of *da'as*. Knowledge's journey from *chochmah* to *da'as* heralds a deepening of existence, and reflects an existential transformation in one's relation to truth. A fact becomes a belief.[20]

The goal of studying divine providence is not merely to understand the information, but rather, to prepare ourselves for the internalization of this knowledge. Indeed, the purpose of all Torah study is to bring the information learned to the level of *da'as*. Proper Torah study serves to internalize wisdom, to make it part of one's essence.

When it comes to the study of divine providence, there is a specific term associated with the internalization of knowledge. Living life with an acute awareness, a real *da'as*, of the reality of divine providence is referred to as having *bitachon*.[21]

---

20. Rabbi Tzadok Ha-Kohen of Lublin remarks in his *Pri Zadik* (*Rosh Hashanah* #9), "The level of *da'as* is achieved through a connection between the brain and the heart, and through this, [the intellect] is realized in the depths of the heart." The Torah itself also relates to the term *da'as* in a similar fashion.

  In the Torah the word *da'as* necessarily implies a connection. It is used to express the ultimate connection between husband and wife, physical intimacy: "And the man knew Eve his wife" (Genesis 4:1). Just as the connection realized through physical intimacy is *da'as*, so too the intense and personal connection between the person and the knowledge he has internalized is called *da'as*.

  Jewish thinkers speak often of the importance of pursuing *chochmah*, of broadening one's knowledge base. But when they describe man's ultimate life mission, they champion the acquisition of *da'as*. The amassing of intellectual knowledge is important, but the completion of man comes through *da'as*, not *chochmah*.

21. The Chazon Ish in *Emunah u-Bitachon* (2:1) explains that people often think that *bitachon* means to believe that only good will happen. This, however, is not real *bitachon*. *Bitachon* means to believe that there is no chance or

The more we understand about divine providence, the stronger our internalized belief will be. With the goal of internalizing the information we study so that it becomes a part of our essence, coupled with our appreciation of living life with *bitachon*, we can embark on the exalted task of seeking to comprehend God's governance of the world: *hashgachah pratis*.

---

happenstance in life, and that divine providence governs everything that happens to man.

Part One

Specific Individual Divine Providence

and

General Species Divine Providence

PART ONE
INTRODUCTION

To what extent does God participate in human activity? Does divine providence extend to beasts of the field, plant life, and inanimate objects?

The first three chapters of this section present and analyze the traditional approach of Jewish thinkers to this esoteric issue. The fourth chapter presents a second, more expansive approach to divine providence. A final chapter outlines common ground between the two approaches, and suggests a reconciliation of their seemingly opposing viewpoints.

We should at the outset familiarize ourselves with some terms. In general, the system of divine providence for an individual is called *hashgachah pratis* and for a group *hashgachah klalis*; however, for the purposes of our study, we need more specialized classifications.

The first term we will use is "specific individual" divine providence. Specific individual divine providence is a system of divine governance that reflects the very close relationship between God's providence and the creations of His world. When God governs with specific individual divine providence, He is directly involved with the most minute details of an individual's life. In this system, God's *hashgachah* is not limited to what impacts an individual physically, but extends to all events that occur in his presence. The fact that an individual observes specific events, or even happens to hear about them, has an intended purpose. This, too, was designed by God, for within this system there is no chance.

The second term we will utilize is "general species" divine providence. General species divine providence is a system in which God's governance relates to a species as a whole. Within such a system, God does not address Himself to the particular individuals of the group, but rather oversees the life of the group as a whole. He insures providential protection for the whole species, but not for the individuals. In other words, in this system, God does not relate to the individuals as individuals, but rather only as they contribute to the greater whole.

Now that we have defined our basic terms, let us proceed.

CHAPTER 1
THE TRADITIONAL APPROACH

H uman beings are governed by specific individual divine providence.[1] This means that every single thing that occurs in an individual's life is ordained by God. Even the seemingly insignificant things happen because God wants them to happen. This approach is well grounded in the literature of Chazal. The Talmud in tractate *Chulin* (7b) states:

> Man does not stub his toe below [i.e., in this world] unless it has been decreed so in Heaven.

This is also the implication of the Talmud in tractate *Erchin*

---

1. At this point we are speaking in general terms. Based on our discussion in later chapters, a sharper and more correct statement would be: Human beings could be governed by specific individual divine providence. As we will develop in those chapters, many thinkers postulate that not all humans, at all times in their lives, are governed by specific individual divine providence.

(16b), which discusses the extent of divinely ordained suffering. The implication is that even those events that have a minimal effect on an individual's life are a result of divine providence:

> How far does the definition of suffering extend? Rabbi Elazar said: [For example,] whoever has a garment woven for him but it does not fit him properly... Even if they intended to mix [one's wine] with hot water, but instead they mixed it with cold, or [they intended to mix his wine with] cold water, but they mixed it with hot water... Mar the son of Ravina said: Even if his shirt was reversed. Rava, or some say, Rav Chisda, or some say Rav Yitzchak, or some say, a *tanna*, taught: Even if one extended his hand into his purse to take out three coins and two came in his hand.

The Rambam notes in his *Moreh Nevuchim* (3:17) that there are no sources in the Bible or Talmud that specific individual divine providence applies to non-humans. Hence, the Rambam advances his theory that only human beings are governed with specific individual divine providence. All other creations — the animals, plants, and inanimate objects — are governed through general species divine providence.

To illustrate this distinction: The death of a specific person is divinely ordained and is a direct result of God's desire for this specific person to die. However, regarding horses, for instance, the life or death of a specific horse is not directly ordained by God. God rather desires for a certain number of horses to die, as he sees fit for the needs of the species or the world. Which horses specifically die is not directly ordained by God.

This view would correctly be called the traditional view, as it is the most popular approach presented by Jewish thinkers from the times of the Rishonim and early Achronim.[2] A careful reading of

---

2. The term Rishonim, "early ones," refers to Jewish scholars who flourished from the close of the Gaonic period (tenth century) through the codification of the *Shulchan Aruch* (fifteenth century). The term Achronim, "later ones," refers to Jewish scholars who flourished from the codification of the

the excerpts below will yield a fuller understanding of the traditional approach. (A thorough study of the original Hebrew passages would be most advantageous to the reader.)

In *Moreh Nevuchim* the Rambam dedicates a few chapters to an exposition of divine providence. In section 3, chapter 17, he outlines four different approaches to understanding divine providence, all incorrect in his opinion, before suggesting his own:

> The first view is the claim of some people that there is no divine providence at all regarding anything in existence, and everything that exists, in heaven and on earth, is merely a result of chance and happenstance. There is no organizer, director, or watchman over anything. This view is pure heresy[3]...
>
> The second view is the opinion of those who believe that over some things there is divine providence, and these are directed by a director and organized by an organizer, but other things are left to chance. This is the view of Aristotle...
>
> The third view is the opinion of those who believe that nothing in existence is a result of chance, not specific individuals nor general groups; rather, everything is with [divine] will, intent, and direction...This view is held by the Muslim school [of theologians] known as the Asharites[4] ...
>
> The fourth view is the opinion of those who believe that all divine acts are a result of a divine wisdom which can bear no injustice [even in regard to animals and inanimate objects]... The Mu'tazilites[5] subscribe to this view...and this view leads them to

---

Shulchan Aruch through the present.

3. Alternative translation: "This is the view of [the ancient Greek philosopher] Epicurus."

4. The Asharite School of early Muslim theology was founded by the theologian Abu l'Hasan al-Ashari (d. 945). The Asharites believed that comprehension of the unique nature and characteristics of God were beyond human capability. They opposed Greek philosophy and were instrumental in distancing Muslim philosophy from Christian philosophy.

5. The Mu'tazilite School of early Muslim theology was originated in eighth-century Basrah, and became the official court belief of the Abbasid

believe absurdities...they will even say about a guiltless mouse that is devoured by a cat or bird that God decreed this fate for this mouse, and God will compensate this mouse in Heaven for what happened...

After reviewing these four incorrect views the Rambam presents his own perspective.[6]

The fifth view is our view, that is, the Torah's view... that man is completely in control of his actions, he has complete free will and acts on his own accord...and everything that occurs to man is fitting to occur...

The Rambam then continues and presents what we are calling the traditional approach.

I believe that divine providence in this lower world, that is under the lunar spheres, is directed towards the human species alone. Only [the human] species is governed [with divine providence] — in every detail [of life], and all good and bad that occurs to him — in accordance with what he deserves... However regarding all other animals, and even more so the plants and other inanimate objects, my view is that of Aristotle. I do not believe at all that this specific leaf falls as a result of divine providence, nor that this spider devours this specific fly as a result of a divine decree on this individual fly. Furthermore, I do not believe that when Reuven spits and the spit lands on a specific mosquito in a

---

Caliphate. Mu'tazilites called themselves *Ahl al-'Adl wa al-Tawhid* (People of Justice and Monotheism) based on the theology they advocated, which expanded on the logic and rationalism of Greek philosophy, seeking to combine them with Islamic doctrines, and show that they were inherently compatible.

6. We will assume that the fifth approach, which he calls "The Torah's view," is the same as the Rambam's opinion, which begins with the words "I believe." It is beyond the scope of this work to address the possibility that the Rambam suggests a sixth approach when he says "I believe." For those interested in further study of the Rambam's opinion, beyond our discussion in this work, be aware that at least three locations in the *Moreh Nevuchim* must be studied: 3:17–18, 3:22–23, and 3:51.

specific place and kills the mosquito, that this was fulfillment of a heavenly decree, nor that when a fish snatches a specific worm floating on the river that such was the will of the Lord. Rather all of the aforementioned occurrences are completely chance, as Aristotle contends.

The *Sefer ha-Chinuch*[7] (commandment 169) takes a similar approach in its discussion regarding the spiritually contracted disease of *tzara'as*:

> The purpose of this commandment is to establish within us that God's providence is specific over every individual human being...
>
> There are groups of people who think that the providence of God is over all species on a specific level, both over humans and over other living creatures. And there are [other] groups who think that God's providence is over all things in the world, whether living creatures or any other things [i.e., even inanimate objects]...to the extent that they think that when one leaf falls from a tree, [God] decreed on it specifically that it should fall... But this [second] view is very illogical.
>
> Then there are evil groups that think that [God] does not operate with providence at all over anything in this lowly world, neither regarding humans or other living creatures. This is the view of the evil and bitter heretics.
>
> However according to what I have heard, we bearers of the true faith [believe] that His providence is over all species of living creatures in a general sense... [But] regarding the human species we believe that [God's] providence is over everyone individually...
>
> Therefore the Torah warned us that when a person is afflicted

---

7. The *Sefer ha-Chinuch* was written in 13th century Spain, although the exact author is a matter of dispute. See the introduction to the Machon Yerushalayim edition of *Sefer Minchas Chinuch* for an extended discussion of the correct authorship. Additionally, see R. Elchonon Wengrov's preface to the second volume of his translation of *Sefer ha-Chinuch*.

with this horrible disease, that is *tzara'as*, he should not assume it to be result of chance, but rather consider immediately that it is a result of his sins.

This approach of the *Sefer ha-Chinuch* is expressed again in its discussion regarding the commandment of sending the mother bird away from the nest (commandment 545).

The purpose of this commandment is to cause us to internalize that God's providence is over the human species on a specific level...and regarding the rest of the living creatures [His providence] is over the entire species on a general level.

The commentary of R. Aharon ha-Levi (Ra'ah)[8] on *Meseches Berachos*, in a discussion of the commandment of sending the mother bird away from the nest, quotes from the author of *Sefer ha-Chinuch*, and records an additional point not recorded in our version of the *Sefer ha-Chinuch*. He adds that the fact that non-humans are governed by general species divine providence, and not specific individual divine providence, may explain the Torah's choice of words in the creation narrative. He writes, "Perhaps this is the sense of what is written [repeatedly] in the account of creation regarding the formation of the animals, beasts, and birds: 'after their kind' (Genesis 1:21, 24, and 25) — meaning, for the continuation of the existence of the species." The Torah's reference to the creation of the other species as following "their kind" teaches that the divine providence that governs non-humans takes the form of general species divine providence (over "their kind") and not specific individual divine providence.

Many other Jewish thinkers also argue the position of the Rambam in *Moreh Nevuchim*, but it would be redundant, perhaps, to include them all here. However, before proceeding we will visit two additional sources that concur with the Rambam's position, for they provide valuable nuanced perspectives, and will therefore be referenced at a later point in our discussion.

---

8.   Spain, d. 1300.

The first source is found in the *Ma'amar ha-Ikarim* of Rabbi Moshe Chayim Luzzato.[9] Rabbi Luzzato writes,

God constantly oversees all His creations, and He sustains and directs them according to the purpose for which they were created. However, because the human species was singled out to receive reward and punishment based on their actions...so too the divine providence they receive is different than the divine providence of other species. That is, the divine providence over the other species is to sustain the specific species according to the laws and boundaries that God desires. Hence, His providence is over each individual member of the each species [only] in regards to its [impact] on the general species...

However regarding the human species, each individual is [governed with divine providence] not only in relation to its [position as a member] of the general species, [but is also] governed with providence as a [specific] individual.

Lastly, let us turn our attention to the writings of Rabbeinu Bechaya ben Asher.[10] In Genesis 18:19 God praises Abraham, "For I have known him, to the end that he may command his children and his household after him, that they may keep the way of God, to do righteousness and justice..." In the context of explaining this praise of Abraham, Rabbeinu Bechaya presents an understanding of divine providence:

"For I have known him"...this is an expression of   divine providence, because God's knowledge of man is His divine providence over him. When the Torah says, "For I have known him," the expression is coming to exclude other people that are not righteous, for the divine providence over them is not like the divine providence over the righteous. You should understand that divine providence in this lowly world over humans takes the form of general species divine providence and specific individual

9.   Italy-Israel, d. 1746.
10.   Spain, d. 1340.

divine providence. There are many verses to this effect, such as, "Great in counsel, and mighty in work, whose eyes are open upon all the ways of men, to give every one according to his ways, and according to the fruit of his doings" (Jeremiah 32:19). However, by other living things, [the divine providence] is general and not specific individual [divine providence], rather only [general species divine providence] to sustain the species.

All of the aforementioned thinkers contend that specific individual divine providence only applies to human beings, and does not apply to other living creatures. However we must note the following qualification: When an animal, plant, or any created entity is owned by a person, or directly impacts the life of a human being, the animal, plant, or created entity may experience specific individual divine providence. However this specific individual divine providence governs the animal, plant, or created entity not on its own account or merit, but only on account of its impact and interaction with a human being. The divine providence is really just an extension of the divine providence of the human being. For instance, since the health of a particular individual's cow directly affects its human owner, that specific cow is governed with specific individual divine providence. God does govern the life of this specific cow as an individual cow, but only because of its direct impact on a human.

This caveat is based on statements of Chazal and can be found in the writings of many thinkers. In *Bemidbar Rabbah* (18:22) Rabbi Chanin of Tzipori relates:

> There once was a scorpion that was on his way to complete a mission from God on the other side of a river. God arranged for him a particular frog that carried him across the river. The scorpion was then able to go and bite a man (who then died).[11]

Based on this, as well as other sources in Chazal, many thinkers adopt this caveat. Rabbi Moshe Cordovero[12] in his encyclopedic

---

11.   In the variant version quoted in *Midrash Tanchuma, Chukas* 1:1.
12.   Israel, d. 1570.

work *Shiur Komah*, writes (section 54, *Hashgachah*):

> When individual divine providence is found in this lower world, even among animals, to save them or bring death upon them, this is not on account of the animal itself, but rather on account of man. And so, if a plague comes and consumes one's grain, it is possible that some of the stalks will be decimated, and some will not, due to the divine will which intends to admonish man... And so when a raven leaves its nest, if it will die or if it will return to its nest, or if a camel will trample it, these [possible occurrences] are not governed by divine providence, unless [the life of this particular raven] will affect the life of a human beings...And so [don't be surprised] if it happens that one lamb, owned by a pious individual, is in a group of lambs in a field, and specific individual divine providence arranges that this one lamb escapes a death which kills all the other members of the flock, like a pack of wolves, or the like, for this [specific individual divine providence] is on account of man and not on account of the lamb.

This view is also espoused by Rabbi David Kimchi (Radak) in his commentary on Psalms. On the verse recited thrice daily in the Ashrei prayer, "Righteous is God in all His ways, pious in all his actions," Radak comments (Psalms 145):

> There is great confusion among the scholarly, for some contend that when a lion tears a lamb asunder, or a similar occurrence, it is a punishment for the [lamb] from God...There are others who contend that there is not [a system] of reward and punishment [i.e., specific individual divine providence] except for the human species alone.
>
> We contend that there is [a system of reward and punishment] for other, non-human species, when it effects mankind... There are other opinions, but they are not worthy of being written.

CHAPTER 2
INCLUSION AND EXCLUSION

The traditional view among Jewish thinkers is that there is a distinction between humans and non-humans regarding specific individual divine providence. However, the issue is slightly more complex. Rabbi Ovadia Seforno[1] explains that this distinction is not necessarily an issue of humans versus non-humans, but rather strikes at the core of what truly distinguishes people from animals. Seforno (Leviticus 13:47) argues that man differs from animals in his ability to emulate God through his actions and in his capacity to develop his intellect to the point of gaining a perception of God. If a person disregards his potential to achieve these goals, he then defaults on his elevated role and denies himself the specific individual divine providence that is reserved for humanity.

For in truth the human species is the ultimate purpose of cre-

---

1.   Italy, d. 1550.

ation, particularly among mortal creations, for [man] alone is predisposed among all creatures to be similar to the Creator in intellect and deed, as God testifies, saying, "In Our image after Our likeness" (Genesis 1:12). Now, this is demonstrably correct regarding all individual humans, through the human cognitive function, which is called "the image of God" [*tzelem Elokim*],[2] and through man's power of free will, which is called "the likeness of God" [*demus Elokim*] — as only man, among all creations, possess free will.

When man is aroused to contemplate the existence of his Creator [and to contemplate] His greatness and goodness — which includes His abundant kindness and truth and how He deals with [mankind] with righteousness and justice — then [man] will walk in [God's] ways, making [God's] will his own. Behold, in this matter he becomes like his Creator more than all other creatures, and this is the ultimate purpose intended by the Creator who brought [all things] into existence, as the verse states, "The righteous one is the foundation of the world" (Proverbs 10:25).

...However those who slumber and are not aware or awakened to know any of these things — such as all the gentiles and a majority of the Jewish nation, except for a few elite individuals[3] — [such people] are then, undoubtedly, under the control of nature and the celestial forces...[and are treated in a fashion] similar to all other living creature who are not governed by divine providence on the specific individual level, but only regarding their general species, because [only] through [the species as a whole] is the intent of God fulfilled.

---

2.   The Rambam in *Hilchos Yesodei ha-Torah* 4:8 states that the definition of the *tzelem Elokim*, "divine image," is not the physical makeup of the body, but rather the spiritual intellect that man has the ability to develop.

3.   This line — "such as all the gentiles and a majority of the Jewish nation, except for a few elite individuals" — is not in all versions of the *Seforno*, and was apparently censored.

Only individuals fulfilling their human potential are granted specific individual divine providence. All others are denying what makes them human, and are therefore governed with the same kind of divine providence as non-humans.[4]

This reasoning that defines a human as one who acts in accordance with his spiritual purpose is also found in the writings of the Ramban. In a sermon entitled *Toras Hashem Temimah*, the Ramban argues that people are distinguished from animals in that mankind ponders existential questions, lives for a purpose, and pines for knowledge of the Creator. Anyone who does not engage in such activities, the Ramban quips, is "no different than the donkey upon which he rides."

> You must know that all knowledge and understanding comes from Torah or comes from the fruits of Torah,[5] and that without Torah man is no different than the donkey upon which he rides... Man, as he is born, lacking a teacher, is like an animal... Even if his mind and intellect lead him to realize, without [the formal instruction of a teacher], that God created the world... [still] he would have no conception of positive acts or sins, nor knowledge or purpose. No deed to him would be more desirable than another. Days and years would be [boringly] similar, in fact,

---

4.   In a later chapter we will discuss the purpose of the system of divine providence. There we will present a further analysis of the *Seforno*'s approach that will explain an additional dimension to divine providence's exclusivity of the Jewish nation.

5.   Rabbi Chavel, in his English edition of the Ramban's writings, *Writings and Discourses*, explains this line from a historical perspective. He notes that when the Ramban wrote this essay, the Torah and Rabbinic literature constituted the principle source of human knowledge — whatever was known of the history of the world stemmed almost completely from the Torah.

　　However, one could argue that the Ramban is also speaking on a deeper level, and is proclaiming that all wisdom in the world is, at its core, a manifestation of Torah. See R. Naftali Zvi Yehudah Berlin's *Ha'amek Davar*, *Bahalosecha*, where he writes that the menorah (its branches and spine) represents all forms of wisdom. It is for this reason that the menorah had to be fashioned out of one solid piece of gold, for all wisdom ultimately has one source — the Torah.

[all of life] would be [boringly] similar, as it is to the animals...

Man [however] was created to recognize his Creator, and if a person doesn't even realize that [God] created him, and especially if he doesn't understand that his Creator considers certain actions better and more preferable, and other actions despised and revolting, then behold man is like an animal, and the purpose of creation is void. The Sages, of blessed memory, have always stated that if the Jews had not accepted the Torah, God would have returned the world to a state of emptiness and nothingness. In other words, if they had no desire to know and learn knowledge of their Creator and that He distinguishes between good and evil, then the purpose of creation of the world would have been nullified...

Don't make a mistake regarding the nations that are situated close to the center of the [civilized] world — like the Christians and Muslims — for they made copies of the Torah and learned it,[6] and when Rome [i.e., the Roman (Christian) empire] spread out to the distant lands, they [i.e., the people of these distant lands] made laws and statutes similar to the Torah.

The Rambam, in the introduction to his commentary on the Mishnah, also advances this theory, defining humanity by distin-

---

6.   It is hard to decipher the correct intent of this line. One reading is that we shouldn't make a mistake and elevate these gentile nations to the level of the Jews based on a perception that they are also inheritors of the Torah, for in truth they merely copied the Torah from the Jews. However, one could also read the line to mean that we shouldn't make a mistake and think that they have no elevated status over the other gentile nations, for in truth, they do have an elevated status due to the fact that they learned some of the ways of Torah from the Jews. No matter which reading is correct, both readings seem to elevate the Christians and Muslims above the other nations. The Ramban's intent is implicit in the rest of the paragraph (not quoted here), especially in his quotation of the Rambam's remarks at the end of *Hilchos Melachim*, chapter 11, that speaks of the cosmic role of these gentile nations in history. Note that in the standard printed edition of the Rambam this section was removed by the censors, but it appears in the first edition (Rome, 1480), and has been restored in the Shabtai Frankel edition.

guishing between people who live in accordance with their intended purpose, and those who squander their potential, chasing the ephemeral pleasures of life.[7]

> Man's ultimate purpose is to perform one function alone, and on account of this function man was created. The rest of his skills are only to sustain him so that he can fulfill that function. This [ultimate] function is: to form in his mind abstract conceptions and to perceive reality as it truly is.

> Common sense dictates that it is absurd and false to claim that the purpose of man is merely to eat, drink, have marital relations, or build mansions — for these are all external ephemeral activities. They do not add to his inner essence. Moreover, these actions he shares with [i.e., are also performed by] many of the other creations.

> However, wisdom is a pursuit that adds to inner essence, and elevates him from a lowly level to an honorable level. Without wisdom he is only potentially a man, but with it he becomes a man in actuality. A person before he uses his intelligence and acquires knowledge is considered like an animal.

> Man is indistinguishable from the other species of living beings except by his power of logical reasoning, i.e., he forms abstract concepts in his mind. And the most exalted abstract concept is perception of the unity of God and all divine ideas that accompany this concept. The other disciplines serve only to train [his intellect] until he attains divine knowledge...

> When man pursues his material desires and his material drive rules over his intellectual essence; when his intellect is enslaved to his material desires to the extent that he returns to be like an animal, which only conceives thoughts of eating, drinking, and physical relations; then the divine potential [i.e., the intellect]

---

7.   Realize we are not necessarily equating the approach of Rambam and Ramban to divine providence for gentiles to the approach of Seforno. We are merely highlighting here their shared perspective on defining humanity in light of the purpose of mankind.

will not be realized, and he will regress as if he is an uncouth beast, stalking through a sea of emptiness...

It is clear from the [above] introductory remarks that the purpose of the world, and all that is in it, is [to produce] the wise and good man.[8] When an individual clearly possesses wisdom and good character traits[9]...and is not steeped in material luxury, and only partakes in material needs to the extent that he requires them for his health and character, such an individual is the purpose and the desired product [of creation].

THOSE WHO SERVE GOD

Until now, we have assumed the view of the Seforno, that not all human beings are granted specific individual divine providence. Only individuals who live up to their human potential, distinguishing themselves from animals through intellect, piety, and thought, are governed with this special level of divine providence.

A similar approach to Seforno is found in a more modern formulation in the writings of Rabbi Eliyahu Eliezer Dessler.[10] He advances the following distinction: Specific individual divine providence is only for the "*oved Hashem*" (individual who serves God), to provide for him all that he needs to serve God successfully; general species

---

8. This statement of the Rambam, that the world was created on account of those who strive for intellectual excellence and a profound knowledge of God, introduces a new perspective to the Mishnaic dictum (*Sanhedrin* 4:5), "Every person is obligated to proclaim, 'The world was created on my account.' " R. Chayim Friedlander in his *Sifsei Chayim* (*Emunah ve-Hashgachah*, vol. 1) suggests in light of this passage in the Rambam that the obligation referred to in the Mishnah is to live a lifestyle that will allow one to honestly make this declaration. Only if one is dedicated to the attainment of wisdom, divine knowledge, and the perfection of character, can one proclaim, "The world was created on my account."

9. The Rambam in a few locations mandates moral perfection as a prerequisite for intellectual and spiritual perfection.

10. England, d. 1953.

divine providence is for the *keilim* (vessels or means) that the *oved Hashem* needs for his service of God. Those who only receive general species divine providence provide a framework for those who are serving God properly. Hence, when God is judging a species, He is, in effect, judging the needs of the righteous individuals who are serving God, and determining to what extent they require this particular species for their purposes. Commensurate to the species' utility for the righteous individuals, God sustains them.[11]

Rabbi Dessler provides an insightful illustration of his theory: In order for a Torah scholar to record his Torah novella he requires a pen. However it makes no difference if he writes with this pen or another pen. There is a need for pens, but not for any individual pen. Hence, when God decides the fate of the world's pens, he merely seeks to insure that there are enough pens in the world to fulfill the needs of those serving God. He does not judge a specific pen, as an individual entity, if it is deserving of continued existence.[12]

Who is included in this group of *ovdei Hashem* of whom Rabbi Dessler speaks? Rabbi Dessler specifically states, "[General species divine providence] is the lot of all the gentiles, as well as Jews that primarily focus on their station in this world." Like the *Seforno* quoted above, R. Dessler excluded gentiles and non-God-fearing Jews from the governance of specific individual divine providence.

This exclusion is also voiced by other Jewish thinkers. Rabbi Cordovero writes (*Shiur Komah*, sec. 54, *Hashgachah*):

> The fourth form of divine providence is [specific individual divine providence] for animals on account of humans. For instance, the story of the scorpion who received specific individual divine providence and was transported across the river [by the frog]...all is sent from heaven. And from here we learn that God

---

11. *Michtav me-Eliyahu*, vol. 2, p. 75–76; vol. 5, p. 308–309.

12. This illustration is brought by Rabbi Dessler's prolific student, Rabbi Chayim Friedlander, in his *Sifsei Chayim* (*Emunah ve-Hashgachah*, vol. 1, p. 25).

orchestrates events to occur, even through a gentile, who are like the animals [regarding divine providence]...

Rabbi Luzzato, in his classic work on Jewish philosophy, *Derech Hashem*, writes (2:4):

When the world was divided into seventy nations, God appointed seventy ministering angels as officers in charge of these nations, to watch over all of their needs. Thus, God does not oversee these nations except in a general manner. It is each one's ministering angel who takes care of the details, through the power that God gives it for this purpose.[13]

It is likely that Rabbi Luzzato's reference to ministering angels that govern the gentile nations is similar to the force we have been referring to as general species divine providence. It appears that the normative system that God established to govern the general species was through the use of ministering angels. An indication to this is present in Rabbi Yosef Ergas'[14] *Shomer Emunim ha-Kadmon* (argument 2, sec. 81). The Midrash (based on a verse in Job 38:33) states, "There is no blade of grass below that doesn't have a constellation [i.e., a heavenly force] above that strikes it and says 'Grow!' " Rabbi Ergas explains the import of this *midrash* as follows:

The first form of divine providence is a general form for all created species in this world that are not destined for [divine] justice. And they are three groups: animals, plants, and inanimate objects. These groups are further divided into many species, as is known. Behold, the mode of their divine providence is through a ministering angel...through this, [the heavenly praises offered by the angels], each of the ministering angels receives a portion of "divine influence" in order to influence [and govern] the generalities of the species over which it is appointed, [and to provide] all the sustenance and other things required for the sustaining of this species..."[15]

---

13. See also the Vilna Gaon's *Aderes Eliyahu*, Deuteronomy 1:6.
14. Italy, d. 1730.
15. The Chafetz Chayim, in *Shem Olam* 1:3, also indicates that the involvement

If gentiles are governed with general species divine providence, then they should also be affected by the caveat that impacts the providential reality of animals and other non-human creatures. As we explained (see chapter 1), when a created entity that is usually governed by general species divine providence directly impacts the life of a human being, that created entity may experience individual specific divine providence in certain circumstances. This specific individual divine providence governs the animal, plant, or other created entity, not on its own account or merit, but only because of its impact and interaction with a human being. According to what we have developed regarding the status of gentiles in the philosophy of most Jewish thinkers, we can conclude that gentiles will receive specific individual divine providence when there is a possible impact on a Jewish individual, or on the Jewish nation.

This conjecture is substantiated in the Bible commentary of Rabbi Meir Leibush, the Malbim.[16] In the first chapter of the book of Jonah, God instructs the prophet, "Arise, go to Nineveh, that great city, and proclaim against it; for their wickedness has come up before Me." In response, Jonah flees from God, seeking to escape the divine imperative. In light of Jonah's stature and saintliness, many commentators seek to explain his disobedience and the inner struggle Jonah faced. As part of his explanation, the Malbim confronts the divine providence afforded the people of Nineveh (*Be'ur ha-Inyan* 1:2):

---

of ministering angels and other celestial forces does not imply a system different from general species divine providence, but rather are the vehicles for that system.

If it is correct that references to ministering angels are another form of general species divine providence, then we can also add the Ramban to the list of thinkers who posit that gentiles are governed only by general species divine providence (something that we will prove in the next chapter), as the Ramban writes in a few places, such as Leviticus 18:25, that the gentile nations are governed via a ministering angel. See also the Ramban in Genesis 28:12 for the possibility that significant segments of the Jewish nation might also be governed by ministering angels.

16. Ukraine-Romania, d. 1879.

"Arise and call out to Nineveh to repent." This mission was not on account of [the people of] Nineveh...for the divine providence of God does not [extend to the gentiles] to send them a prophet, for [this is the case] only with regards to the Jewish nation. However, the divine providence of the [people of Nineveh] was on account of the Jewish nation, since the kingdom of Assyria [where Nineveh was the capital] was destined to be God's rod of wrath [i.e., God's tool] to smite the Jewish nation (who were condemned [by God]). Hence, God wanted [the people of Assyria] to repent so that they would be able [i.e., spiritually worthy] to fulfill the decree against the Jewish nation... God wanted to show that Assyria had merits that exceeded [the merits of] the Jewish nation, for they listened to the words of the prophet and repented, and the Jewish nation hardened their necks [based on Kings II 17:14]. When Jonah realized that calamity for the Jewish nation would sprout from his mission, he schemed ways to elude the mission. He decided it would be better to take his own life [by throwing himself] in the sea than to be the cause of calamity for the Jewish nation.

The divine providence that evoked a mass repentance was afforded the inhabitants of Nineveh not on their own account, but only because of the cosmic role they needed to fill vis-à-vis the Jewish nation.[17]

---

17. Radak also suggests that the divine providence that governed the inhabitants of Nineveh was not directly related to the Assyrians themselves. His suggestion is more universalistic, focused less on the Assyrian nation's impact on the Jews, and more on the their impact on society at large.

"Arise and go to Nineveh; call out to her [inhabitants], for their evildoing has risen before me..." We learn from here that God governs even the gentile nations when their evil, treacherous behavior grows. So too we see with the generation of the deluge and the people of Sodom: "For the land is filled with treacherous behavior" (Genesis 6:11). [God here governs even the gentiles] since treacherous behavior ruins society, and God desires the settlement of civilization. However, regarding other sinful activity, [the gentiles] aren't bad enough [in God's eyes] that He [bothers to] govern them, only with the Jewish nation, as it says in the

Two Solutions

Our approach presents a startling conclusion that needs to be addressed. All of the individuals governed by general species divine providence seemingly exist only to facilitate the small number of Jews who faithfully serve God. Yet when one considers how many non-God-serving individuals there are in the world — in comparison with God-fearing Jews — it is challenging to accept this reality.

This question was asked, in a slightly different context and fashion, by the Rambam in the introduction to his commentary on the Mishnah (quoted above). The Rambam was not writing about divine providence per se, but about the importance of pursuing knowledge and developing one's intellect, while limiting one's involvement with material base pleasures. To the Rambam, this is man's ultimate purpose, differentiating him from animals, and entitling him to the benefits of humanity.

Towards the end of his discussion, the Rambam raises an issue similar to the one we are addressing: There are so many people in the world who neither pursue wisdom nor abandon materialism. How could that be the purpose of man's existence, if such a large segment of the population is completely removed from this endeavor? Moreover, the Rambam establishes, as we read in the above quotation, that all of creation — including people who forfeit their elevated mission — was created for the purpose of the individuals who acts in accordance with the divine will for humanity. Hence, we are faced, according to the Rambam, with the quandary: How can there be such a disproportionate amount of entities (people, animals, plants, etc.) created for the express purpose of the few?

There remains in this matter the following question that one might ask. It has been said that God [lit. the divine wisdom] does not create anything in vain, and everything has a purpose.

---

prophecy of Amos, "For only you have I known among all the families of the earth" (Amos 3:1).

Furthermore, of all the creations that are in this world [lit. below the lunar sphere], man is the most exalted. [Additionally,] man's purpose is to form in his mind abstract concepts. If so, why did God create so many people...? We observe that most people are lacking in cleverness, empty of intelligence, and only desire to fulfill their material desires. The wise man who despises worldly [pleasures] is alone among many.

The Rambam suggests two answers to his question. His first is that God created all of these individuals in order to assist, and provide a physical atmosphere for, those individuals who pursue a life of service to God. The Rambam argues that the God-serving individual will only have time to fulfill his mission if there are many other people around dedicated to the pursuit of the mundane, hence providing that individual with his daily needs.

> [The purpose of creating those individuals who do not apply themselves to elevated goals] is for them to assist the individual [who does]... Man lacks many things and has many needs. He would have to learn plowing and harvesting, [how] to thresh, grind, bake, and fashion tools for all of the aforementioned tasks, in order to produce with them his nutritional needs. Similarly, he would have to learn spinning and weaving in order to weave his clothing. He would also have to learn how to build in order to construct a place of shelter, and to fashion tools for all of these labors. Not even the lifetime of Mesushelach[18] would suffice to learn all of these tasks that a person necessarily requires for sustenance. When would he find time to study and acquire wisdom? Therefore, all of those people were created to perform these acts, which are needed in a civilization...so that the world is settled and wisdom found therein.

The Rambam's answer is, in a sense, the underlying principle of our approach. The solution he proposes to the question of why so many people were created is: because that is how many people it

---

18.   Who lived 969 years (Genesis 5:25).

takes to provide the proper context for the accomplishment of the dedicated. God, in His infinite wisdom, assesses the exact number of individuals required in order to provide the proper environment for those who do seek the Divine.

The Rambam suggests an additional solution. He maintains that the masses of people were also created to provide a social framework and society for the few individuals who pursue the acquisition of wisdom and a life of service to God. Everyone, the Rambam argues, needs camaraderie. Even the small number of God-fearing individuals need other people, and the many inhabitants of earth are necessary to provide human interaction and "remove [the potential for] depression from the wise ones."[19] Interestingly, he adds, "You may consider this to be of small value, but still it is necessary and more significant than the first [answer, i.e., to provide the material needs for the elite few]."

EACH ENTITY ACCORDING TO ITS PURPOSE

Perhaps we can suggest a slight reorientation of who is fulfilling human potential as it pertains to divine providence, and through this modified approach suggest another answer to the aforementioned question of the Rambam.

We have already explained how all gentiles and many Jews are lacking in the fulfillment of their human potential, and consequently are governed by general species divine providence instead of specific individual divine providence. Therefore we were faced with the question of why God would create so many people for the

---

19. This is not the only occasion where the Rambam stresses the importance of environment, as it pertains to one's sense of existential comfort and happiness. In his introduction to tractate *Avos, Shemoneh Perakim*, chapter 5, the Rambam underscores this idea, describing how depression inhibits one's growth. Additionally he prescribes tactics for an individual to combat feelings of existential despair that can impede his intellectual and spiritual development.

purpose of assisting the few. Yet, perhaps, one could question the assumed status of gentiles as it pertains to our discussion. Many non-Jews live an enlightened life. They follow the seven Noachide commandments required of all mankind and seek to develop a relationship with the Creator of the world. If such an individual seeks righteousness and justice, cares for his fellowman, and lives humbly while earning an honest livelihood, perhaps he too is fulfilling the will of his Creator and would merit, on some level, specific individual divine providence.

A cogent argument can be made for this approach in the sources we have examined. Rabbi Luzzato, in his *Ma'amar ha-Ikarim*, chapter 1, opened his essay with the following statement:

> God constantly oversees all His creations, and He sustains and directs them according to the purpose for which they were created.

For what purpose were the gentiles created? Is it necessary for them to convert and become Jews? Perhaps a gentile fulfills the "purpose for which he was created" by living honestly, seeking an existential understanding of life, and following the seven Noachide commandments as expressions of God's will.[20]

Based on this perspective, we can suggest the following modified approach: Specific individual divine providence is reserved for those who are fulfilling their purpose in this world as individuals, while general species divine providence is for those who are fulfilling their

---

20. We should note that our discussion here addresses the generalities of classifying gentiles and should be understood as a philosophical direction and not a statement of halachic reality. For indeed, on a practical level, a gentile may need to undergo a formal procedure to rise to the elevated status we are now discussing. For example, the Rambam in *Hilchos Melachim* (8:10–11) discusses the status of a *ger toshav* and requires a gentile to formally accept the seven Noachide laws in the presence of a *beis din* of three. According to the Rambam, a gentile is only accorded this elevated status if he keeps the seven Noachide laws because God commanded them to Moshe and not if his impetus for keeping them is his heightened sense of morality and good will.

purpose in this world as a group. When it comes to animals, plants, and inanimate objects, the choice for which divine providence will govern them is not in their control. However, when it comes to humans, both Jew and gentile, the power to determine in what way they will be governed is completely in their own hands.

If an individual chooses to act in accordance with God's will, and fulfill his intended purpose, as it differs for Jew and gentile, then he will merit specific individual divine providence.[21] But if one chooses to reject his divinely charged purpose, and instead engages only in activities that he shares with the animals (eating, drinking, physical relations, and other material pursuits), then he will receive only the form of divine providence reserved for non-humans. The choice is up to man.[22]

Support for this approach can be mustered from the fact that various Jewish thinkers accord certain gentile groups elevated statuses. The Ramban, in his essay *Toras Hashem Temimah*, quoted above, specifically defined the Christians and Muslims of his day — as opposed to other gentile nations — as occupying an elevated

---

21. This is not to imply that their merited providence will necessarily be equal. In the next chapter the issue of varied levels of specific individual divine providence will be addressed.

22. This may be the intent of the Rambam in *Moreh Nevuchim*, where he argues that specific individual divine providence is granted based on one's level of intellectual perfection, service of God, and dedication to the purpose of humanity.

> The amount of divine providence that governs an individual is commensurate to the share of [divine] influence that he achieves through his inborn abilities and [intellectual/spiritual] accomplishments. Therefore, the extent of divine providence is not the same for each individual human. The varying levels of providence upon them is like the varying levels of their individual perfection... This is one of the foundational points of the Torah.

> The Rambam's language always refers to "human beings." Nowhere does the Rambam distinguish between Jew and gentile in his discussion; only between those fulfilling their roles and those who default on their responsibilities.

status. This was the result of the fact that they adopted elements of the Torah into their religious identity.[23]

An unprecedented classification of certain gentile groups is advanced by Rabbi Menachem ha-Meiri,[24] in his *Beis ha-Bechirah*. In numerous locations the Meiri argues that the strict Talmudic laws governing interaction with gentiles only address the unorganized tribal religions of pagan society, "who possess no form of religion whatsoever, and do not humble themselves to any fear of the divine."[25] However, "nations bound by the strictures of a religious system" are not to be included in many of the restrictive laws of the Talmud. This category of "nations bound by the strictures of a religious system" is the Meiri's novel method of distinguishing between the barbaric pagan nations of Talmudic times and the more progressive gentile nations of his own day.[26]

---

23. We are suggesting that certain gentile groups can theoretically be accorded an elevated status due to their adherence to the Noachide laws. It is beyond the scope of this work to define the monotheistic status of Christianity and Islam, a necessity since rejecting idolatry is one of the Noachide laws.

24. France, d. 1316.

25. Meiri, *Beis ha-Bechirah*, *Avodah Zarah* 15b.

26. The Meiri's comments in *Bava Kama* 37b imply that inclusion in the category of "nations bound by the strictures of a religious system" is dependent on adherence to the seven Noachide laws, which includes the rejection of idolatry. If so, the inclusion of Christianity is dependent on the halachic debate regarding the status of Christianity as a monotheistic religion.

    Yet, it appears that the Meiri intended to include Christians in the category of "a nation bound by the strictures of a religious system," and not only because, in *Avodah Zarah* 2a and 6b, the Meiri implies that Christians specifically are excluded from the restrictive laws in place for idol-worshipping nations. From various places in his writings, it emerges that the Meiri's true distinction is not between idol worshippers and monotheists, but rather between barbaric unorganized tribal religions that typically engage in gross idolatry, and civilized nations with organized religious systems that do not generally partake in extreme idolatrous practices. It is the presence of an organized religious system that provides for an elevated culture, where a sense of culpability for one's actions exists along with a concrete impetus to act morally.

The Meiri's attitude toward "nations bound by the strictures of a religious system," and their consequential elevation from the denigrated status of gentiles in the Talmud, provides us a theoretic construct to grant certain gentile groups an elevated status.[27]

The fact that the Ramban and the Meiri elevated the status of certain gentile groups notwithstanding, it may still be presumptuous to suggest that not all gentiles are excluded from specific individual divine providence, considering that so many Jewish think-

---

This understanding of the Meiri's distinction is consistent with, and augmented by, his comments elsewhere. In *Avodah Zarah* 22a he describes the idolatrous nations as those who acted "with disgusting behavior and contained repulsive elements," while the modern nations "are clean from these repulsive elements, and to the contrary, they punish such behavior." Similarly, in *Avodah Zarah* 15b the Meiri stresses that the barbaric nations "do not humble themselves to any fear of Heaven…and are not careful to avoid sin," and in *Shabbos* 156b the Meiri stresses how a religious system causes a person to assume responsibility for his actions.

Therefore, the Meiri's dispensation could be in place for Christianity, as an organized system of religion, even if their Trinitarian views are not completely monotheistic. This tension – that the Christians are not pure monotheists, yet they possess a more elevated status than the early pagans – may underlie the Meiri's comments in *Bava Kama* 113a, where he includes in the category of "nations bound by the strictures of a religious system" those who worship God "in any way, even if their faith is far from ours"; and in *Gittin* 62b where he includes those "who believe in the existence of God, His unity, and His ability, even if they err in some [beliefs]."

It should be noted that the Meiri does not claim that all modern nations have an elevated status, and he admits that there are modern-day nations that are no different than the early barbaric nations.

27. The Meiri's position is not quoted often in halachic literature. For an example of a modern day application of the Meiri's position, see R. Eliezer Waldenberg (Israel, d. 2006), *Tzitz Eliezer* XV:47. However, there were great Jewish scholars who discouraged referencing the Meiri's view. See *Kovetz Sh'elos u-Teshuvos Chassam Sofer* 90. It should be noted that the Meiri also seemingly makes this distinction between the barbaric gentiles of the Talmud and the more enlightened modern nation in a non-halachic discussion; see *Beis ha-Bechirah, Shabbos* 156a and *Chibur ha-Teshuvah, Shever Gaon* 1:1 and 2:6.

ers explicitly excluded them. It is fitting to readdress some of these sources in light of our suggestion.

The *Seforno* quoted at the beginning of this chapter stated:

Those who slumber and are not aware or awakened at all to know any of these things, such as all the gentiles and a majority of the Jewish nation...[are treated in a fashion] similar to all other living creatures who are not governed by divine providence on the specific individual level.

It could be that Seforno is not saying that gentiles are inherently excluded from specific individual divine providence. Rather, he states that they are excluded because they "slumber and are not aware or awakened at all to know any of these things." What if they were to awaken? Do they happen to slumber or is their stupor inherent to who they are? Note that Seforno also excludes a "majority of the Jewish nation" from specific individual divine providence. Just as a "majority of the Jewish nation" are not intrinsically excluded from specific individual divine providence and most definitely have the potential to achieve such governance, it would follow, perhaps, that the gentile nations are also not intrinsically excluded. Accordingly, we can understand that Seforno's comments were a description of circumstances prevalent in his day, and perhaps were not meant to be understood as a denial of a gentile's ability to experience an elevated level of divine providence.[28]

The reorientation we are suggesting presents the possibility that there are more people governed by specific individual divine providence than originally thought. Moreover, this approach also sheds light on a corollary issue: Why are there so few people who are pursuing an elevated existence? Why don't more people join the

---

28. The Rambam in *Mishneh Torah, Hilchos Shemittah ve-Yovel* 13:13, who refers to "*kol ba'ei olam*," may be a source that gentiles have the ability to acquire an extremely elevated spiritual status. If this source includes gentiles, it certainly indicates the ability of gentiles to be governed by specific individual divine providence.

elite few?[29]

We can now better understand the disproportionate amount of people in existence that are divorced from specific individual divine providence and live in a manner incongruous with the divine will: God does not create the overwhelming masses devoid of specific individual divine providence. The choice is given to man, who has within his own power the ability to rise from the depths of bestiality and live truly as a human. Moreover, there may be more people than we realize fulfilling their purpose in this world. The ultimate judge of humanity, of who is living in accordance with the expected level of conduct and intellectual achievement — who is an *oved Hashem*, and who is not — is God alone.

A Special Distinction

The previous section addressed the exclusionary approach voiced by many Jewish thinkers to the status of gentiles vis-à-vis specific individual divine providence. We struggled with the seeming exclusion of the overwhelming majority of mankind from specific individual divine providence, and sought ways to consider the inclusion of many gentiles.

We would now like to suggest an additional perspective for confronting the exclusion of gentiles from specific individual divine providence. Unlike the above approach, this perspective will maintain the literal exclusion of all gentiles from the system of specific individual divine providence. We must first briefly explore another element of divine providence, for it contains an additional, and crucially important, facet to understanding the already complex picture of specific individual divine providence.

The system of specific individual divine providence undoubtedly

---

29. Until now we have been addressing why there are so many people around who do not receive specific individual divine providence. Now we ask, why are there so few who do?

exists for countless purposes. By attempting to understand the purpose, aim, and goal of specific individual divine providence we can arrive at a clearer understanding of why it may only apply to certain individuals. But before embarking on this task, we must note the care and caution that the greatest Jewish thinker exercised when broaching this topic. Man, by definition, cannot grasp the complexities of God's design, and must always be guided by intellectual humility when suggesting purposes and reasons behind God's initiatives. Even conclusions arrived at by the greatest human minds are but mere suggestions, and without a doubt, do not capture the entire picture.

This being said, various suggestions appear in the literature of Jewish thinkers to explain the purpose of specific individual divine providence. It can be suggested that God's governance through specific individual divine providence is on account of his love for humanity, and his desire to interact with his creations. Just as a parent wishes to not only experience a child's development from the sidelines, but also to be an active participant in his or her child's life, so too God desires to actively participate in the lives of His creations.

Another suggestion is made that specific individual divine providence clears a path for one's spiritual growth by imbuing daily life with meaning. If one lives with an acute awareness that everything that transpires in one's life is directly orchestrated by God and is intended exclusively for that person, then every event, every happening, abounds with meaning. Mishaps are transformed into harbingers of calamity, evoking sincere repentance, while success resulting from important decisions are imbued with religious import, and serve as further encouragement. Introspection becomes the operative response to happenings, and mundane actions are impregnated with significance.

If love and repentance were the only goals of specific individual divine providence, the fact that many Jewish thinkers divorce the gentile nations, as well as many Jews, from the governance of specific individual divine providence would require additional explana-

tion. Do we not say thrice daily in the *Ashrei* prayer that God has
compassion on all His creations, "God is good to all, and merciful
to all of His creations?" (Psalms 145:9). Is it not God's will that
the wayward among us, Jew and gentile alike, abandon their sinful
ways, and return wholeheartedly to Him?

Thus, we must introduce an additional purpose for specific individual divine providence that will, coupled with our discussion
until this point, help further our understanding of who is governed
by specific individual divine providence.

We will return to the first source quoted in this chapter, the
view of the Seforno. The Seforno explains in the remainder of the
aforementioned quotation that the Jews were chosen by God as the
conduit of His divine message to mankind, and as such, the Jews
were bequeathed the holy Torah, charged with the responsibility to
safeguard its statutes, and entrusted with the challenge of serving
as a "light unto the nations" (Isaiah 42:6, 49:6). To insure that the
Jews live up to this formidable and challenging cosmic role, God
established a system of divine providence to remind them to stay
the course.

> [God] chose the Jewish nation as it says, "Hashem, your God,
> has chosen you to be His own treasure" (Deuteronomy 7:6).
> This He did because the hopefully intent of God was more likely
> to be realized among the men of this nation than among other
> nations, for the existence of God and His unity was known par-
> tially and accepted among all [of the Jews] from their ances-
> tors…He [therefore] wrote and taught them the Torah, which
> is the intellectual portion, and [instructed them regarding] the
> commandments…He then warned that if they deviate from the
> path, He would awaken their ears through suffering, as it says "If
> you will listen…I will put none of these diseases upon you, which
> I have put upon Egypt" (Exodus 15:26).

Besides the insight Seforno's comments provide us regarding the
purpose of divine providence, we also gain a newfound understanding of why specific individual divine providence may only apply to

a small few. Since Jews alone are charged with the mission of bringing God's message to the world, only they are in need of specific individual divine providence to insure that they do not "deviate from the path." The gentile nations, who do not play the cosmic role entrusted to the Jewish nation, are therefore removed from the system of divine providence on a specific individual level.

Living according to the general rules of nature, and not experiencing specific individual divine providence, is not a punishment for plants and animals. Nature is the physical reality of the general world, and all those who operate in the general world are under its dominion. However, those who realize their divine potential and, striving for a transcendent existence, seek to infuse the mundane world with spirituality by spreading the light of Torah, are afforded the special distinction of governance through specific individual divine providence.

• • •

What emerges from the sources and discussions in this chapter is that our original distinction between humans and non-humans, presented as the traditional view, may in fact have further complexities. It appears that even among humans, not all humans are governed by specific individual divine providence. We have also suggested that even the further distinction between Jews who are serving God and the rest of mankind may not be the complete picture.

CHAPTER 3
LEVELS AND GRADATIONS

After discussing which individuals are governed by specific individual divine providence, we now turn our attention to further complexities and delineations within this group. As we have explained, certain individuals are afforded the governance of specific individual divine providence, based on their dedication to the divinely ordained goals of mankind. Even within this group of committed persons we find levels and gradations. Those fully committed to their spiritual imperative experience a heightened level of specific individual divine providence, those less committed experience less.

Rabbeinu Bechaya, in his commentary on the verse "For I have known him, to the end that he may command his children and his household after him, that they may keep the way of God, to do righteousness and justice..." (Genesis 18:19), addresses the highest level of specific individual divine providence:

Individual divine providence that governs people is divided into two categories. [The first is] divine providence over man to know in detail all of one's actions and thoughts. [The second is] divine providence over man to protect him and save him from the influence of chance.

The divine providence to know in detail all of one's actions applies to all Jews and non-Jews, as is stated in the verse, "He that fashions the hearts of all [man], that considers all their doings" (Psalms 33:15). But the divine providence to save one from the influence of chance is not with all individuals, not even all Jews, rather only with the righteous Jews, for God saves the righteous ones from chance happenings — which all other people are subject to. God does not forsake His righteous ones, and He does not remove His sight from them, rather His divine providence governs the pious one constantly, [His providence] does not depart from them at all. This is the expression "for I have known him,"[1] that specific individual divine providence is upon him, and the other righteous ones, to save them from the chance occurrences of humanity. This is the view of the Ramban..."

The statement of the Ramban to which Rabbeinu Bechaya refers is also on this verse. All the Ramban writes is the following cryptic statement:

In my opinion, the correct interpretation of this verse is: a real knowledge of him. This teaches us that God's knowledge — which is His divine providence in this lowly world — guards over the general laws. And also humans are left to the influence of chance, until their appointed time arrives. However, with His

---

1. Perhaps it is based on these remarks of Rabbeinu Bechaya, and the following comment of the Ramban, that the Malbim interprets the verse in Amos (3:2) — "You only have I known of all the families of the earth..." — as a reference to divine providence. As the Malbim writes:

    "You only have I known" — this expression appears at times regarding God and refers to a heightened level of His divine providence [for the righteous] since they are connected to His knowledge. Such as in the verse "For I have known him, to the end that he may command his children..."

pious ones, [God] concentrates to know him on an individual level, to have His guard cling to him constantly. [God] does not remove His knowledge and consciousness of him at all.

The Ramban's opinion is expressed more fully in his own words in his commentary on the book of Job. Commenting on the verse, "He does not withdraw His eyes from the righteous" (Job 36:7),[2] the Ramban writes:

> It is also for this reason that God guards the righteous ones, for when their eyes and hearts are always with Him, so too the eyes of God are upon them "from the beginning of the year till the end of the year"(Deuteronomy 10:12). [This relationship is true] to the extent that the completely pious individual, who is constantly clinging to Him and never disrupts his total devotion to Him for mundane matters, will be guarded always from all chance occurrences, even the happenings of nature. He will be saved from them all — as miracles will constantly occur on his behalf... According to his closeness (to God) he will be protected with the highest level of protection. However, he who is distant from God in thought and deed, even if he isn't deserving of death due to his sins, is [nonetheless] left to chance.

Accordingly, only those who demonstrate complete devotion to God and their divine mission in this world are governed by unabated and uncompromising specific individual divine providence. These elevated individuals are protected from all occurrences of chance and happenstance. Every step they take is watched over, and directed, by God. The implication being that those who display less of a commitment and dedication are governed by specific individual divine providence to a lesser degree.

---

2.   This verse is one of the two alluded to by the Ramban in his Torah commentary on Genesis 18:19, quoted above. Interestingly, the Ramban is more forthcoming and less esoteric regarding this issue in his commentary on Job than in his Torah commentary.

Indeed the Rambam explicitly advanced this theory in his *Moreh Nevuchim* (3:18):

> The amount of divine providence that governs an individual is commensurate to the share of [divine] influence that he achieves through his inborn abilities and [intellectual and spiritual] accomplishments... Therefore, the extent of divine providence is not the same for each individual human. The varying levels of providence upon them is like the varying levels of their individual perfection... This is one of the foundational points of the Torah.

Based on the Rambam, Rabbi Yosef Albo, in his *Sefer ha-Ikarim* (4:10), also endorses this view:

> It follows that divine providence should attach to man in a greater degree, in accordance with the superiority of his intellect (over that of the lower animals)... It follows that he who perfects his intellect, as much as his ability allows,[3] will enjoy a greater degree of divine providence than one who has not done so. On the other hand, he who does not perfect his soul at all and wastes his intellectual energies is reduced to the degree of lower animals and loses divine providence altogether.

The pious and righteous individual, who is "constantly clinging to [God], and never disrupts his total devotion to Him for mundane matters," is removed from the influence of chance and happenstance. However what is the status of the less committed? To what extent does specific individual divine providence govern those who are committed to the divine goals of mankind, yet are not situ-

---

3. This important phrase, "as much as his ability allows," is crucial as it suggests that there is subjectivity in "intellectual perfection." Accordingly, an individual's "intellectual perfection" is not judged based on quantity (how much he knows), but is rather assessed based on an individual's God-given ability and his own personal effort. Hence, intellectual perfection for a person like the Rambam would require much more "information" than the intellectual perfection of a regular person would, unless that person had the ability to be like the Rambam. The battle for intellectual perfection is waged between man and himself.

ated on the sublime level of those pious individuals described by the Ramban and Rabbeinu Bechaya? It is regarding this class of people we will now address.

The statement of the Talmud in tractate *Chulin* 7b has already been quoted, "Man does not stub his toe below [i.e., in the world] unless it has been so decreed in heaven," as was the statement from tractate *Erchin* 16b, "How far does the definition of suffering extend..." What emerges from these Talmudic statements is that even the smallest things are governed by specific individual divine providence. Are these Talmudic statements only addressing the pious individuals of whom the Ramban and Rabbeinu Bechaya speak? Without a direct qualifying statement accompanying these passages, the answer to this question is hard to determine.

In truth, it would be foolish egotism to try to systematically describe the exact extent of specific individual divine providence for this group as a whole. Just as no two people are exactly the same in appearance, so too they differ in their level of commitment to the divine goals of mankind. Different upbringings, experiences, influences, social class, and other innumerable factors, all contribute to the unique existential makeup of an individual. And hence, the relationship with God and the fabric of one's spiritual identity differs from person to person. This, in turn, dictates varying levels of providential governance, commensurate to each individual's spiritual station. Even if we provide an overall classification for these individuals' specific individual divine providence, we do so realizing the inherent shortcomings of such an undertaking. With this in mind, let's begin our attempt to understand more deeply the system of divine providence.

THE INFLUENCE OF CHANCE

The Ramban, in his above referenced cryptic comments to Genesis 18:19, writes, "And also humans are left to the influence of chance, until their appointed time arrives." Who are these humans left to the influence of chance? One could argue that the Ramban here is merely referring to those who are governed by general species divine providence, as delineated in the previous chapter. However, the context of the Ramban does not necessarily suggest such an interpretation.

It is very likely that this group who are "left to the influence of chance" are the people we are currently discussing: those committed to the divine goals of mankind but not situated on the level of the pious righteous individuals who experience unabated specific individual divine providence in every minutia of life. Ostensibly this would mean that while certain, and perhaps most, events are governed by specific individual divine providence, there are times when a person can be harmed, or affected, by the influence of chance and happenstance.

The concept of being "left to the influence of chance" is also found in the Rambam's *Moreh Nevuchim* (3:51), where he certainly claims that it even applies to those individuals normally governed by specific individual divine providence.

He who is perfect in his perception, who never averts his focus from God, is governed constantly by divine providence. [However] one who is perfect in his perceptions, but at times turns his attention away from God, is governed by divine providence only while he meditates on God; providence is removed from him when he is involved with other matters... When one averts his attention from God, when he is separated from God — and God is therefore separated from him — then [such an individual] is exposed to any evil that might befall him... Behold, I have explained to you that the reason a human being is left to chance and exposed to destruction, [in a fashion] similar to animals, is due to his being separated from God. However one who has "God in his heart" (Kings I 3:28) is not touched by any evil whatsoever.[4]

---

4.   In *Moreh Nevuchim* 1:23–24 the Rambam equates being "left to the influence of chance" with the removal of divine providence. Besides the Ramban and the Rambam, others also make references to God leaving man to chance. For instance, in *Shiur Komah*, sec. 54, *Hashgachah*, Rabbi

This idea of being "left to the influence of chance" raises a fundamental question. On a practical level, I think we assume that most individuals are not "perfect in perception," nor can they claim to "never avert focus from God." And so, when is one to ascribe daily occurrences to divine providence, and when can one assume that what transpired was merely a result of chance?

Before we address this practical problem, we need to address a more fundamental issue that arises from our explanation of the Ramban's cryptic comments. The Ramban makes many statements in his writings that imply that there is no system of nature or existence of chance. The most famous is in his Torah commentary on Exodus (13:16):

> From the overt major miracles man comes to a realization of the hidden miracles,[5] which are the foundation of the Torah. For a person has no portion in the Torah of our teacher Moses unless he believes that all our matters and circumstances are miraculous, that they do not follow nature or the general course of the world — this is true regarding the nation and the individual.[6]

Cordovero writes:

> [God, at times,] removes His divine providence, leaving man to chance, as in the verse, "And I will surely hide My face on that day..." And this is the state of most of our dealings with the world nowadays in exile.

5.   The concept of "hidden miracles" appears often in the Ramban. See, for example, Genesis 17:1, Exodus 6:2, and many other locations. Hidden miracles are miracles that do not flagrantly break the natural course of events, and instead operate within the "laws of nature." For example, in Genesis 17:1 the Ramban says a hidden miracle may be a family surviving a national famine, or a soldier escaping death in battle. The *Sefer Me'or ve-Shemesh* (Genesis 30:2) of Rabbi Kalonymus Kalman Epstein (Poland, d. 1823) defines hidden miracles as all miracles that man can deny and dismiss as mere nature. Hence, a hidden miracle may be a righteous farmer experiencing ample rain for his produce and personal health and happiness for his family, while the splitting of the sea during the Exodus from Egypt was not a hidden miracle.

6.   See the Ramban's essay *Toras Hashem Temimah* for a more elaborate discussion of this issue.

Without a system of nature, chance occurrences are impossible. Chance is defined as "an unknown and unpredictable element in happenings that seems to have no assignable cause."[7] These events that "seemingly" have no assignable cause obviously must have some cause. When a flowerpot falls from a window, or a person jams a finger, the cause must either be divine, a result of God's orchestration — or natural, a result of the laws of physics, human psychology, etc.

If the Ramban maintains that there is no system of nature, in that everything that happens is divinely ordained, how can the group of people we are currently addressing be "left to the influence of chance" and happenstance?

REDEFINING CHANCE

The resolution of our issues is as follows: What the Ramban calls being "left to the influence of chance" is also a form of specific individual divine providence, and the word "chance" as it is colloquially used is not what the Ramban means when he uses the word.

That "chance" for the Ramban does not mean a haphazard system of existence that lacks divine providence is implicit in the Ramban's statement in his Torah commentary on Deuteronomy 11:13:

> You should know that miracles are not performed, whether for good or bad, except for the completely righteous or completely evil individuals. However regarding ordinary people, the way of the world (*minhago shel olam*) orchestrates for them good and bad, according to their actions.

The last line of the Ramban's comments seems to be self-contradictory. If ordinary people are governed by nature and the "way of the world," then they aren't dealt with "according to their actions." And if things are orchestrated "according to their actions" then how is it considered "the way of the world"?

---

7.   The American Heritage Dictionary of the English Language, 4th ed.

The answer is that being "left to the influence of chance," or to the influence of nature, or to "the way of the world," is also a form of specific individual divine providence.

However, even if being "left to the influence of chance" is also a form of specific individual divine providence, it is clearly different from the unabated specific individual divine providence that is reserved for one who is "who is perfect in his perception" and "never averts his focus from God." What is the difference between these manifestations of specific individual divine providence? How does the providence of one who is "left to the influence of chance" differ from the higher form of unabated providence?

NATURE AND DIVINE WILL

Before presenting one possible perspective for viewing these different systems, let's first address a relevant theological issue.

The Ramban, throughout his writings, takes issue with those who contend that after God created the world He removed his direct interaction, leaving the governance of the world to a system of nature. In his commentary on Exodus 13:16, the Ramban addresses the historical significance of major overt miracles, such as the splitting of the sea in the Exodus narrative. In this context the Ramban writes that through the overt miracles one comes to a realization of God's hidden miracles, i.e., the daily governance of the world. The Ramban's intention in Exodus 13:16 is to disprove the view that the world runs on its own natural course.

However, this does not necessarily mean that there is no system of nature. To explain, God established at the dawn of creation that whenever a rock would be thrown up it would always fall down, unless He has a specific reason to alter the fate of the rock. God created this "rule" as a pattern for His will. Obviously, He does not have to follow this pattern, but in general He does. This pattern, this normal behavior, is the Ramban's definition of what we call nature. Every time a rock is thrown up, God actively wills the rock to fall down, and this constant will, which almost always follows the same pattern, is the normal course of events. After observing this pattern for a while, a person may forget that God is in fact willing the rock to fall each time. But, if God occasionally wills the rock to float upwards, instead of falling, one immediately realizes that all the previous times that the rock fell it was because God was actively willing it to fall.

As a further illustration, if Reuben begins to tap his forehead, an observer is obviously aware that it is Reuben's will to tap his forehead, and that Reuben could start and stop whenever he wishes. However, imagine if when the observer enters the room Reuben is already tapping his forehead. The observer leaves and returns an hour later, and Reuben is still tapping his forehead in the same manner. If this would continue for hours, days, or weeks — every time the observer chances into the room Reuben is tapping his forehead — eventually the observer would start to think that this action is uncontrollable. Perhaps Reuben has a spasm or a condition that is beyond his control. What else would account for the non-stop tapping over such a long period of time? However, if during the fourth week of observing such activity, Reuben would stop tapping his forehead and begin snapping his fingers, it would be clear that all the previous tapping was merely a reflection of Reuben's constant will.

The Ramban in Exodus 13:16 is not denying a system of nature. God most definitely has a pattern of will that He normally implements, and it is called nature. What the Ramban is stressing is that this natural pattern is a reflection of God's ever-present will and governance, not an independent system that runs on its own.[8]

Hence, the Ramban's statement in Genesis 18:19 condemning certain individuals to chance does not contradict his denial of nature in Exodus 13:16. As we saw clearly in Deuteronomy 11:13, the Ramban states that both chance and nature operate within the sys-

---

8.   There may be a pattern called nature, but there is no "mother nature."

tem of divine providence. Being "left to the influence of chance" is not a reference to a haphazard system of nature, but merely refers to a different manifestation of specific individual divine providence.

The practical question, raised above, of whether any given incident is God's will or is just a natural occurrence, now falls by the wayside. Man is not forced to figure out when to ascribe daily occurrences to divine providence and when to assume that what transpired was merely a result of chance, for everything is a result of specific individual divine providence.

MERITING DIVINE INTERVENTION

Now we can attempt to explain how being "left to the influence of chance" is also specific individual divine providence.[9]

There is a concept in the Talmud called *makas medinah*. *Makas medinah* literally means a national plague, and it refers to a situation where God makes a condemning decree against a community or nation. In such a case the individual members of the community lose their individual identities and are subject to the same fate as their fellow community members. This is true even if they themselves, as individuals, are not deserving of the impending punishment; by dint of their membership in the community they are subject to the community directed divine decree. The Talmud (*Bava Kama* 60a) affirms this reality when it states "once the angel of death is given permission [to kill] it doesn't distinguish between good and evil."[10]

---

9. This explanation may raise as many questions and it answers, and we must admit that it is only the beginning of an answer. This disclaimer having been stated, we reiterate that, according to the Ramban, being "left to the influence of chance" is specific individual divine providence, even if we cannot completely explain how and why. In a later chapter we will return to this issue and offer another perspective. However, the following explanation is important to state at this stage of our discussion.

10. This reality is evoked by the Talmud to explain why the Jews in Egypt had to worry on the night of the plague against the Egyptian firstborns. The Talmud there also advises against an individual venturing outside his

The only exception to the fate of a *makas medinah* is the completely pious individual. If one is completely righteous and pious, so then God may intervene to save him from the fate of his fellow community members.

This dispensation is developed by Rabbi Moshe Cordovero in *Shiur Komah* (sec. 54, *Hashgachah*):

> *Makas medinah*, described in the Talmud as the few affecting the fate of the many...is true only regarding one who isn't completely righteous; however, one who is [completely righteous and] outstanding in action [still] receives his individual divine providence and is saved from all that transpires.

Rabbi Cordovero continues and brings, as an illustration, a case of a righteous individual traveling on a ship in the ocean. Due to the presence of sinners on the ship, a divine decree is issued that the ship will sink. Rabbi Cordovero writes that the fate of the individual is dependent on his level of righteousness. One righteous person may be righteous enough that he would not have died had he not been on this ship, but since he now finds himself in this dangerous situation, he will die on account of the decree against the ship and its travelers. A more righteous individual may be saved through divine intervention, on account of his heightened righteousness, even though a decree has been meted out against the ship. If he is even more righteous, his possessions may also be saved. However, the most righteous individual will not only be saved individually, but on account of his extreme piety and righteousness, will cause the entire ship to be saved (so that he forgoes any inconvenience).

It can be argued that when the Ramban says man will be "left to the influence of chance," he means that the course of events — whether the natural pattern normally implemented by God or a

---

home during times of disease for the same reason. Moreover, this concept introduces additional facet of meaning to the famous adage "Woe to the wicked man and woe to his neighbor" (originally from *Mishnah Nega'im* 12:6, but more popularly known from tractate *Kiddushin* 40a, and *Avos de-Rebbi Nasan* 9:1).

makas medinah — will be able to affect him. God will not intervene and alter the normal pattern; he will not intervene and protect the individual from the decree against the larger group.

According to this understanding, an individual "left to the influence of chance" is an individual who would not merit a personal divine intervention to protect him against the fate of his surroundings.[11] He is similar to the first individual described by Rabbi Cordovero in the illustration of the ship at sea: he suffers the fate of his fellow seamen even though he would not have been injured had he not been on the ship.

If an individual suffers hardship, and is not saved from calamity, it may be an indication that the individual was not righteous enough to merit divine intervention. Had he been on a more elevated level, perhaps divine intervention would have protected him.[12] In a sense it was divine providence that this individual did not experience divine providence. Being "left to the influence of chance" means that it was divine providence — God's assessing of the situation and finding the individual's righteousness wanting — that this individual did not experience divine providence, i.e., God's intervention to save him.

In other words, specific individual divine providence is always the determinant of what transpires in one's life. Sometimes specific individual divine providence dictates that God will intervene on one's behalf, and other times specific individual divine providence dictates that God will not.

• • •

---

11. As stated above, we will return to this concept of being "left to the influence of chance" in a later chapter and deepen our understanding of this lofty concept.

12. It is presumptuous and foolish to offer specific reasons or to suggest a lack in righteousness when a person suffers hardship or experiences tragedy in a real life situation. It should be obvious that our discussion here is merely theoretic in nature, and that there could be other factors involved in a person's suffering. For instance, the Talmud's famous description of *yesurim shel ahavah* is another viable option to explain calamity. See also *Kiddushin* 40b.

What emerges from our discussion is that there are varying levels of specific individual divine providence. The pious righteous individual, who is constantly meditating God's ways and is completely dedicated to the divine goals of mankind, enjoys the protection and guidance of God's providence at all times. Those less dedicated, who at times interrupt their intellectual bond with God and disregard their elevated goals, are "left to the influence of chance." However this does not mean that man is divorced from specific individual divine providence, as there is no such thing as a haphazard system of nature. One perspective of leaving to chance is a reduced form of providence that actively dictates that the normal pattern of the world will not be altered on this individual's behalf. The individual's seemingly being left to chance is itself a reflection of the specific individual divine providence that governs him.

CHAPTER 4
THE EXPANSIVE APPROACH

T he traditional view that we have developed until now is reflected in many sources and represents the view of many Jewish thinkers,[1] yet there are other sources and thinkers that argue that specific individual divine providence also extends to non-humans.

The Talmud in tractate *Chulin* 63a describes the *shelach* bird that would fly over bodies of water and swoop down, snatching fish out of the water for food. Regarding this *shelach* bird, the Talmud relates: "When Rabbi Yochanan would see a *shelach* bird he would exclaim, 'Your judgments are as deep as the sea.' " Rashi[2] comments in the name of his teacher, "That You [God] arrange for the *shelach*

---

1. The list of thinkers who endorse this view includes, but is not limited to, the Rambam, Ramban (to be discussed further in this chapter), Chinuch, Rabbeinu Bechaya, Radak, Ramchal (Rabbi Luzzato), and Remak (Rabbi Cordovero).

2. Rabbi Solomon ben Yitzchak (France, d. 1105).

bird, who carries out judgment and acts with vengeance on Your be-half among the fish of the sea, to kill those proscribed for death."

The implication of this Talmudic statement is that the death of specific animals is governed with specific individual divine provi-dence. Indeed, the Radak (Psalms 145:17) notes that this seems to be the interpretation of this Talmudic statement, even though he himself disagrees with this approach.

Another important source for this more expansive view of spe-cific individual divine providence is in *Bereishis Rabbah* (79:6):

> Rabbi Shimon ben Yochai and Rabbi Elazar, his son, hid in a cave for thirteen years during a period of persecution, and they [sustained themselves by] eating inferior dried-out carob[3] until their skin became like a *chaludah* [i.e., dried out and cracked]. After thirteen years they exited and sat at the entrance of the cave. They saw a hunter hunting birds. When Rabbi Shimon would hear a heavenly voice declare, "Free! Free!" [the bird] would es-cape [from the hunter's trap]. When he would hear the heavenly voice declare, "Death" [the bird] would be trapped and captured. [Rabbi Shimon] proclaimed [that these heavenly voices serve to teach] that "even a bird isn't captured without a [decree] from heaven; how much more so, the life of a person."[4]

Rabbi Shimon ben Yochai therefore deduced that he should leave the cave, and his survival would be wholly dependent on God.

Based on this source from *Bereishis Rabbah*, many thinkers argue that specific individual divine providence governs not only the lives of human beings, but extends to the lives of animals. Rabbi Eliyahu of Vilna,[5] the Vilna Gaon, arrives at this conclusion in his com-

---

3. Alternative translation: Carob from a place called Gerudah.

4. This account also appears with slight variation in *Talmud Yerushalmi, Shvi'is* 25b. Interestingly, the above quote from *Chulin* 63a is attributed to Rabbi Yochanan — the same Rabbi Yochanan who was responsible for compiling the *Talmud Yerushalmi*.

5. Lithuania, d. 1797

mentary on the *Zohar, Yahel Ohr* (*Shelach* 157b). He writes:

> Even the way of nature (*hanhagas ha-teva*) is directly controlled by God's judgment and divine providence. "For man does not jam his finger below, unless it was so decreed in heaven" (*Chulin* 7b), and even a bird is not trapped without a decree from above. However nature is the messenger [of this heavenly decree]. For when it is decreed that this one will become wealthy and this one destitute, God arranges it that this one misplaces his money and this one find it. He does not cause a miracle that money is instantly generated [for one person] and for the other the money floats away to heaven. This is nature.
>
> As a parable, a king sits in his palace and from his vantage point can see a man and animal off in the distance. He can send wheat food to the man through a series of different schemes, and barley food to the animal in a similar fashion. They only see the cause immediately preceding their reception of food, and they think this [visible] reason is the sole reason they received food. So too, the king may have a trap set, and when the time arrives the king sets off the trap and the passerby is caught by the neck and dies. The fool imagines that an unfortunate accident has occurred to him, but this too is simply "nature" bringing about "poisonous food."[6]

The Vilna Gaon's equation between human beings and birds in the first paragraph, and the man and animal featured in the parable are indications that he is of the opinion that all creatures, human and non-human, are governed by similar specific individual divine providence.[7]

---

6. I.e., just as the healthy wheat was in actuality a direct result of the king's intervention, so too the murderous trap is a direct result of the king's machinations.

7. From the above quotation, one may understand that the Vilna Gaon extended his expansive view of specific individual divine providence only to animals, such as the bird featured in the story with Rabbi Shimon bar Yochai. Does his expansive view also include plants and inanimate objects?

This conclusion is also expressed by Rabbi Tzadok ha-Kohen Rabinovitz of Lublin,[8] in his work *Pri Tzadik* (*Emor* 3):

> Behold all things occur due to divine providence from God, even beasts and other living creatures are not governed by chance, Heaven forbid, as it is taught in the Yerushalmi, "When Rashbi (Rabbi Shimon ben Yochai) would hear a heavenly voice declare 'Free!' [the bird] would escape..."

There are difficulties, however, using the *Bereishis Rabbah* source as a proof that non-humans are governed by specific individual divine providence. The supposed individual divine providence for this bird may not have been on account of the bird itself as an individual, but perhaps on account of the hunter as an individual. The individual providence experienced by this bird may merely have been an extension of the specific individual divine providence of the hunter (see the end of chapter 1). Indeed, Rabbi David Luria,[9] the Radal, advances this argument in his commentary on *Bereishis Rabbah*:

> This [Midrash] teaches that there is specific individual divine providence even with animals. However, perhaps [this is not the case] since this [occurrence of] trapping is really a human issue

---

Some suggest that in his other writings, the Vilna Gaon hints that he in fact understands that all created things, even plants and inanimate objects, are governed by specific individual divine providence. One example is in his commentary on *Tzafrah de-Tzniusa*, where he writes:

> The general rule is that all that was, is, and will be till the end of days is included in the Torah, [from the words] "In the beginning" until [the words] "to the eyes of all of Israel." This is not only true regarding generalities, but every minute detail of every species, and every individual person, everything that will happen to him from the day of his birth until his end, in every reincarnation — every detail and every detail of a detail. And so too with all species of beast and animal, and all living things that are in the world, and every blade of grass, plant, or inanimate object — all the details and details of details of every species, and the individuals of each species, until the end of days, and that which will happen to them...

8.   Poland, d. 1900.

9.   Lithuania, d. 1855.

— the gain of the hunter is dependent on [the capturing of the bird].

Additionally, it could be argued that the heavenly voice served to teach Rabbi Shimon a lesson, namely, "even a bird isn't captured without a [decree] from heaven, how much more so, the life of person." It could very well be that the heavenly decree was not on account of the bird at all, but to instruct Rabbi Shimon to leave the cave.

The possible difficulties suggested above notwithstanding, many thinkers, nonetheless, use this account in Bereishis Rabbah as a source that specific individual divine providence extends to non-humans. In addition to the Vilna Gaon and Rabbi Tzadok of Lublin, noted above, Rabbi Yonasan Eibeschutz,[10] in his *Ya'aros Devash* (2:6), also adduces support for this position from the *Midrash Rabbah*:

> From the perspective of *mazel*, the Jews should be lost from the world, Heaven forbid, and it is through the grace of God that He doesn't give us over to the system of *mazel* at all. However, this is true only if we don't attribute [our survival] to chance. [This will not be the case, and God will give us over to chance] when we do attribute [our survival] to chance and say "this one died from old age"... See the Rambam's opinion in his *Moreh Nevuchim*, where he states that regarding humans God governs with specific individual divine providence; over animals and birds, He doesn't govern with specific individual divine providence, but rather [in general] with the whole species. [But] the Ramban disagrees.
>
> This [issue lies at the center of] a statement by Chazal in *Midrash Rabbah*: When Rashbi left the cave, he saw a hunter hunting a bird, and a voice was heard that it should not be trapped, and [the bird] was not trapped. And regarding a different bird a voice was heard that it should be trapped, and it was trapped. Rashbi said, "We see that a bird is not trapped unless there is a heavenly decree."

---

10.   Germany, d. 1764.

We should try to understand what [Rashbi] thought originally. Originally he thought like the Rambam in the Moreh that over individual birds [God] does not govern with specific individual divine providence. Afterwards, he thought like the Ramban that even over individual birds His divine providence is specific and individual, and [Rashbi] understood that a bird is not trapped without a heavenly decree.

Nowadays, due to our many sins in exile, God has hidden His face from us, as is written "I will surely hide..." (Deuteronomy 31:18), and behold, we are basically like animals and birds — according to the view of the Rambam — that we experience no specific individual divine providence. This is the statement of David, "I watch, and have become like a bird that is alone upon the roof," for we are like a solitary bird, who experiences no specific individual divine providence.

Most perplexing is Rabbi Eibeschutz's assertion that the Ramban contends, contrary to the view of the Rambam, that specific individual divine providence extends to non-humans.[11] Indeed, all indications from the writings of the Ramban imply that he agrees with the Rambam's limitation of specific individual divine providence to the human species alone.

First, the Ramban in his commentary on Genesis 18:19, quoted above, seems to present his view differently than Rabbi Eibeschutz suggests.

This teaches us that God's knowledge — which is His divine providence in this lowly world — guards over the general laws. And also humans are left to the influence of chance, until their appointed time arrives...

When the Ramban writes that God's divine providence in this world is "to guard the general laws," he is ostensibly referring to

---

11.   I later found that this perplexity is also noted by Rabbi Yitzchak Stern in footnote 59 of his introduction to the 1964 Lemberg edition of the *Sefer Shomer Emunim ha-Kadmon* by Rabbi Yosef Ergas.

non-humans. This is clear from his next sentence, where he states, "And also humans are left...," implying that the previous statement was not referring to humans. Additionally, Rabbeinu Bechaya, commenting on this verse, states:

> You should understand that divine providence in this lowly world over humans takes the form of general species divine providence and specific individual divine providence... However, by other living things, [the divine providence] is general, and not specific to the individual, rather only [general species divine providence] to sustain the species... This is the view of the Ramban.[12]

A clearer indication that the Ramban agrees with the Rambam is found in the Ramban's discussion of the proliferation of idolatry in the generation of Enosh (Exodus 13:6). The Ramban delineates various groups of heretics, and in one classification, the Ramban endorses the Rambam's approach that animals are not governed with specific individual divine providence.

> There were also those who admitted to God's knowledge, but denied divine providence, thus equating man with the fish of the sea — who are not governed [with divine providence]...

However, the strongest proof of the Ramban's opinion is the Ramban's own words in his commentary on the book of Job (36:7).

> This verse explains an important concept regarding divine providence, and is the topic of many verses [in the book of Job]. Men of Torah and complete faith believe in divine providence, that God oversees and guards human beings individually, as is written [concerning God], "Great in counsel, and mighty in work, Whose eyes are open upon all the ways of man, to give every one

---

12. It should be noted that Rabbeinu Bechaya does postulate an additional theory regarding divine providence, following the one quoted and before his statement: "This is the view of the Ramban." Hence, one could argue that this later statement only refers to the second theory and not the one we are discussing. However, a careful reading of the Ramban and Rabbeinu Bechaya reveals that both theories Rabbeinu Bechaya presents are based on the Ramban.

according to his ways, and according to the fruit of his doings" (Jeremiah 32:19).[13]

...We do not find in the Torah, or in any prophecy, that God oversees and guards the other non-speaking species individually; rather, regarding them He guards only the general species, as they [fill their role] as part of the universe [lit. the heavens and earth].

It is clear and well known that it is due to man's recognition of his Creator that [God] deals with man providentially and guards him. This is not so regarding the other creations, which do not speak and do not recognize their Creator. [14]

In case it isn't clear from the Ramban's language that he supports the view of the Rambam, the Ramban ends his discussion saying: "The Rambam has explained this [concept] well in his book, *Moreh Nevuchim.*"

• • •

The fact remains that there are Jewish thinkers of the opinion that specific individual divine providence extends to non-humans. In addition to the above quoted thinkers, many Chasidic masters also espouse this view.

Rabbi Menachem Mendel of Vitebsk[15] in his work *Pri ha-Aretz* (*Bo*) writes:

It is hard for evil people [to believe], and their hearts reject [the belief], in specific individual divine providence — that no per-

---

13. Rabbeinu Bechaya, in his *Kad ha-Kemach* (*Hashgachah*), explains that the first half of this verse, "Great in counsel, and mighty in work, Whose eyes are open upon all the ways of man," refers to the principle of general species divine providence, and only the second half of the verse, "to give every one according to his ways, and according to the fruit of his doings," refers to the concept of specific individual divine providence.

14. See also Ramban's comments to Job 3:1.

15. Russia, d. 1788.

son jams his finger, and no blade of grass dries out and is up-rooted, and no rock is strewn about, unless it is the destined time and place for such an event to occur...all is from God, and serves to reveal His Godliness, wisdom, and attributes...

Imrei Pinchas, a collection of sayings of Rabbi Pinchas Shapiro,[16] the Rebbe Pinchas of Koretz, one of the preeminent students of the Ba'al Shem Tov, records the following declaration:

A person must believe that even the straw resting on the ground, [is there] due to heavenly decree. He decreed [that the straw should lie] there [specifically], with this end here and that [end] there.

Like all major Chasidic doctrines, this view is ascribed to the founder of Chasidism, Rabbi Yisrael Ba'al Shem Tov,[17] as seen in this quotation from the work *Shomer Emunim* (*Ma'amar Hashgachah Pratis*, chapter 17), written by the founder of the Toldos Aharon community of Jerusalem, Rabbi Aharon Roth.[18]

It once happened that the holy scholar [lit. bright light], our teacher, the Ba'al Shem Tov, may his merit serve as protection for us, was in a field with his students. All of a sudden, a strong wind blew and many leaves fell from the trees onto the ground. [The Ba'al Shem Tov] said, "My sons, know that this wind that just passed this instant was due to a specific worm that was situated on one of the leaves. The sun was shining particularly strongly [on this worm], and [the worm] cried out to God. God sent this wind, which blew many leaves to the ground, and this leaf [with the worm] was one of those leaves." The Ba'al Shem Tov shared this with them, to inform them of the extent of specific individual divine providence, and how [God's] mercy is upon all of the world's creations.

---

16. Russia, d. 1791.

17. Ukraine, d. 1760.

18. Israel, d. 1947.

This expansive view, championed by the followers of the Ba'al Shem Tov, has been passionately promulgated in our times with extremely strong declarations. A series of anonymously authored pamphlets was distributed in Jerusalem in 1992, titled *Ani Ma'amin*, addressing issues of faith from a Chasidic perspective. In the third pamphlet, subtitled *B'zos Ani Bote'ach*, the author quotes an incredible statement in the name of Rabbi Simcha Bunim of Peshischa.[19]

> Once, the Rebbe, Rabbi Bunim of Peshischa, may his merit serve as protection for us, was taking a stroll with his holy followers through a field. [During the stroll] he threw himself to the ground and picked up one grain of sand. He raised it in the air, and then returned it to the same spot in the ground. He then said, "He who doesn't believe that this grain of sand needs to be specifically in this spot, due to the specific individual divine providence of God, is considered a heretic, Heaven forbid!"

An equally sensational declaration was pronounced by the Chasidic giant Rabbi Chayim Elazar Shapira,[20] Rebbe of Munkatz, in his seminal collection of responsa, *Minchas Elazar*. In section 1, *responsum* 50, the Munkatzer lists important works that will serve as "a beginning of wisdom" for one who wishes to pursue the study of Kabbalah, "the wisdom of truth." Of the books he suggests, one is the monumental work *Shomer Emunim ha-Kadmon* of Rabbi Yosef Ergas.[21] Although he has much praise to shower upon the work of

---

19. Poland, d. 1827.

20. Hungary, d. 1937.

21. *Shomer Emunim ha-Kadmon* is a polemical work, written in the form of a debate between a talmudist and a kabbalist, that advocates and provides a basic introduction to the study of kabbalah. *Shomer Emunim ha-Kadmon* is so fundamental to the novice kabbalah student that when the rabbinic leaders of Poland instituted a ban, in 1756, to restrict the study of kabbalah as a response to the heresies of Shabtai Tzvi and Jacob Frank, they gave the *Shomer Emunim ha-Kadmon*, as well as two other works, a special status. The *cherem* (ban) stated:

> We have seen the need to establish a protective boundary and organize a proper order in response to those who wish to trample a path to God,

Rabbi Ergas, he is bothered by the *Shomer Emunim ha-Kadmon*'s approach to divine providence, and he expresses his reservations:

> However at the end of the work *Shomer Emunim*, in his discussion of divine providence, one should skip [the relevant discussion], and [moreover] it is forbidden to read it...for he has established general and specific principles [on the topic of divine providence] that are against our faith...[for we believe] that specific individual divine providence from God extends to each and every detail, even to the smallest thing. However the rest of the [*Shomer Emunim ha-Kadmon*] is very pleasant.

The "problematic" discussion is nothing more than a presentation of the traditional approach to specific individual divine providence. It is found in the *Shomer Emunim ha-Kadmon* in argument 2, section 81:

> The details of the different forms of divine providence and their reasons, I see fit to separate into ten categories, as I have seen in the works of kabbalists, specifically *Sefer Elimah*.[22]
>
> The first form of divine providence is a general form of divine providence for all created species in this world that aren't destined for [divine] justice. And they are three groups, animals,

---

and are overly zealous to ascend the divine chariot...they go out to collect the lights of the secrets of the Torah before they are able to read the [written] Torah of God intelligently; [they can't even] understand the simple explanation of the Gemara... Therefore we decree, with the power of the curses mentioned above, that it is forbidden for any person to learn from them [i.e., kabbalistic works] — even those writings that are known with certitude to be the authentic works of the Ari, with no errors — [still] there is a definite prohibition for any person to learn from them before the age of forty...only the *Zohar*, *Shomer Emunim*, and *ha-Pardes* of the Ramak, *z"l*, all have the same status, that from the age of thirty and on, one may learn from them, on condition that they are printed and not handwritten...[and] even one who has reached forty, "not all who wish to assume the name may assume it" (*Berachos* 2:8), but only one who is well versed (lit. filled his stomach) in *Shas* and *Poskim*.

22. *Sefer Elimah* was written by Rabbi Moshe Cordovero, and contains the same ten categories that appear in his *Shiur Komah*.

plants, and inanimate objects, and these groups are further divided into many species, as is known...all these things are governed by divine providence on the general species, by the ministering guardian appointed to it. However specific individual divine providence, such as if this ox will live or die, if this worm will be saved or trampled, if this spider will prey upon this fly, and all similar details, is beyond the purview of the power of the ministering guardian to govern. All animals, and definitely all plants and inanimate objects, are not governed [with specific individual divine providence] on issues like this, for their aim is achieved only through their species, and there is no need for the individuals to have divine providence. Therefore, everything that relates to the individuals is completely left to chance, and not decreed by God, unless it has an impact in any way on the providence of man, as we will explain soon.

The second form of divine providence is providence over the human species, where each person is governed by God with absolute individuality...

What is most fascinating about these statements of the Chasidic masters is that there are many Rishonim, as we have seen, who disagree with this Chasidic approach, and would certainly not be considered heretics by the Rebbes of Peshischa and Munkatz. This fact is obviously not unknown to these Chasidic scholars, and is noted by Rabbi Shapira in the endnotes to the *Minchas Elazar*, called *Kuntres Sheiri Minchah*, where he admits that the view he is espousing argues with many earlier Jewish thinkers:

That which I have written [against the *Shomer Emunim ha-Kadmon*] is not an opinion I have reached on my own. Therefore, do not be surprised, my dear [student], if you find statements regarding divine providence similar to his [i.e., the *Shomer Emunim ha-Kadmon*] in older works. For I have received a tradition from righteous and pious individuals who received from our teachers and fathers, their merit should serve as a protection for us, that everything is from God alone, without any chance, even the most minute detail.

This intellectually honest, yet semi-apologetic, tone found in the *Kuntres Sheiri Minchah* is also featured in other Chasidic writings. As a group, the Chasidic thinkers disagree wholeheartedly with the traditional approach; however, many acknowledge the need to justify their position, realizing that traditional Jewish thought advocates the Rambam's position. Hence the *Divrei Chayim*, the famous work of the Sanzer Ruv, Rabbi Chayim Halberstam,[23] adds the following disclaimer after expressing his view of specific individual divine providence (*Divrei Chayim, Miketz*):

> Granted that the Rambam has a different opinion regarding this issue, but the view of Chazal [is as I have written] that even a bird is not trapped without providence from above...[24]

In a slightly sharper tone, Rabbi Dov Baer Schneersohn,[25] son and dynastic heir of Rabbi Shneur Zalman of Liadi, the founder of Chabad Chasidism, writes in his *Derech Chaim* (*Sha'ar ha-Teshuvah* 9):

> [Based on what we have explained] it is possible to commend those who attack the Rambam on the topic of divine providence, that he maintains there is a differentiation, i.e., that specific individual providence only applies to humans, and not to animals, plants, and inanimate objects...In truth, divine providence is on

---

23. Poland, d. 1876.

24. Interestingly, the editor of the newly published *Divrei Chayim* adds a footnote to this statement that says: "This [statement about the bird being trapped] is quoted by *Tosefos* in tractate *Avodah Zarah*..." It appears that the editor is attempting to garner support for the *Divrei Chayim* from the fact that this statement is quoted by *Tosafos* in *Avodah Zarah* 16b (s.v. *dimus*). However, it appears that *Tosafos* there does not quote this statement in regards to its theology, but is merely quoting this account in order to shed light on the definition of the word *dimus*. As *Tosafos* say quite clearly in the beginning of their remarks: "*Dimus* is an expression of mercy, as we see in the *Yerushalmi Shvi'is* regarding an incident when Rabbi Shimon ben Yochai..."

25. Russia, d. 1827.

all creations, even the plants and inanimate objects, for behold, "He grants sustenance to all flesh" (Psalms 136:25), and in His kindness he sustains and provides for [all creatures] from the horns [of wild oxen to the eggs of vermin] (*Shabbos* 107b)...

• • •

One might mistakenly assume that the kabbalistic underpinnings of the Chasidic movement is solely responsible for this more expansive view of specific individual divine providence championed by the Chasidic masters. This assumption would also explain the Gaon of Vilna's departure with the traditional view of the Rishonim, as the Gaon's teachings are known for their kabbalistic content. However, this mistaken assumption oversimplifies a most complex issue. Many towering figures of the kabbalah world have indeed embraced the view of the Rambam. For example, Rabbi Moshe Cordovero, in his kabbalistically laden work *Shiur Komah*, which we have previously encountered, dedicates a detailed essay to an analysis of divine providence. In his introductory remarks, he cogently argues the view of the Rambam:

> The first form of divine providence is general species divine providence. It includes all types of animals and plant life, and definitely people, to maintain them, provide sustenance for them, and insure their vitality, for these are the necessities of the species. The sustaining of the species includes insuring the birth process [of animals], or germination [of plant life], and all other relevant processes...
>
> The second form of divine providence is specific individual divine providence over people, regarding the good and bad that occur to their children and livestock, and [regarding] financial success. All is overseen with divine providence — whether to increase their bounty due to righteousness, or to decrease their wealth because of evildoing. This divine providence is increased for the pious ones and those who fear God. Such individuals ex-

perience divine providence even over their vessels, their pots and pans, and all of their property, both for good fortune and bad.

In addition to Rabbi Cordovero, we have already noted the views espoused by other thinkers entrenched in the study of kabbalah, such as the Ramban, Rabbi Luzzato, and Rabbi Ergas. These prolific thinkers, giants in the world of kabbalah, whose writings are replete with kabbalistic teachings, did not follow the view later articulated by the Chasidic masters.

CHAPTER 5
BRIDGING THE GAP

We have seen that there are two distinct approaches to specific individual divine providence. The traditional approach, first stated by the Rambam in his *Moreh Nevuchim*, argues that specific individual divine providence only applies to human beings, while all non-humans are governed by general species divine providence. The more expansive view, espoused most prominently by the Vilna Gaon and the Chasidic masters, argues that every creation, animate and inanimate, human and non-human, is governed by specific individual divine providence.

In this chapter we would like to suggest that these views might not be contradictory. Realize that the undertaking to reconcile these seemingly different views is not merely out of a desire to simplify the issue. For in truth, we are forced to seek out reconciliation, for many of the aforementioned Jewish thinkers seem to contradict themselves in their writings, at times embracing one approach and at times the other. Clearly, as we have stated throughout, the issue is deeper than it appears.

We have already quoted in chapter 1 Rabbi Moshe Chayim Luzzato's *Ma'amar ha-Ikarim* where he endorses the Rambam's approach.[1] Rabbi Luzzato repeats this understanding in his work *Derech Hashem* (2:4:8).[2] However, in his monumental work dedicated to a discussion of the unity of God, *Da'as Tevunos* (I:36), he writes that specific individual divine providence extends to all creations:

> He who believes in God's unity, and understands its concepts, has to believe that God is one, individual, and unique. He has nothing preventing Him [from doing anything] at all, no [other] source in any way or any fashion. Rather He alone is completely in control... He alone governs all of creation with specific individual divine providence. Nothing in this world is born unless it is a result of His will and handiwork, and [nothing is the result of] chance, nature, or constellations.

This internal contradiction is also found in the *Shomer Emunim HaKadmon* of Rabbi Ergas and appears in a span of a few paragraphs (argument 2, section 81). Rabbi Ergas first makes the following statement:

---

1. The quotation from chapter 1 reads:

    > However, because the human species was singled out to receive reward and punishment based on their actions...so too the divine providence they receive is different than the divine providence of other species. That is, the divine providence over the other species is to sustain the specific species according to the laws and boundaries that God desires... However, regarding the human species, each individual is [governed with divine providence] not only in relation to its [position as a member] of the general species, [but is also] governed with providence as a [specific] individual.

2. R. Luzzato writes:

    > When the world was divided into seventy nations, God appointed seventy ministering angels as officers in charge of these nations, to watch over all of their needs.
    >
    > Thus, God does not oversee these nations except in a general manner. It is each one's ministering angel who takes care of the details, through the power that God gives it for this purpose.

First of all you should know that there is nothing that occurs by chance, be it an insignificant or significant [event], and even the system of "nature" is directly from God — for [nature's] secret is [God's] name Elokim, which is the *gematria* (numerical value) of *teva* (nature). There is no creation [that was created] by chance, without direct intent and divine providence.

However, a few paragraphs later, Rabbi Ergas adopts the opposing view:

The first form of divine providence is a general form of providence for all created species in this world that aren't destined for [divine] justice. And they are three groups, animals, plants, and inanimate objects, and these groups are further divided into many species, as is known... All animals, and definitely all plants and inanimate objects, are not governed [with specific individual divine providence], for their aim is achieved only through their species, and there is no need for the individuals to have [specific individual] divine providence. Therefore, everything that relates to the individuals is completely left to chance, and not decreed by God...

The second form of divine providence is providence over the human species, where each person is governed by God with absolute individuality.

Faced with the above internal contradictions in the writings of Jewish thinkers,[3] we are forced to delve deeper into the issue. While

---

3. Others have noted apparent internal contradictions in the writings of other Jewish thinkers. We have chosen, however, to omit mentioning these contradictions in the body of the text, as we feel that they are readily explained and do not strengthen our point (of noting contradictions). For the sake of thoroughness, however, they are quoted here:

    The *Sefer ha-Chinuch*, which commented in commandment 169 that the expansive view of divine providence is "very removed from human reason," seems to make a contradictory statement in commandment 21:

    [The Exodus from Egypt] is a full indication and proof of the creation of the world...that there is a pre-existent God with will and power who gives all created things their being... [the Exodus] must permanently

it is obviously possible that the different approaches are in disagreement, as the simple reading of the sources indicates, it is nonetheless appropriate to also consider that there is no disagreement.[4] Below we will outline a philosophic construct that will enable us to begin to explain how the two views are not completely at odds with each other. We will also revisit some of our sources and suggest more accurate readings based on our new, and deeper, understanding of the concepts of divine providence.

We will develop our philosophic construct in three stages:

Stage I: Overt and Hidden Divine Providence

One may argue: All creations are governed by specific individual divine providence and general species divine providence. When many Jewish thinkers write that only committed humans are governed by specific individual divine providence, and not other humans, animals, plants, and inanimate objects, they mean that from man's perspective they do not appear to experience specific individual divine providence. In the parlance of these thinkers, governance

---

affirm human faith in the knowledge of the eternal God, and [the faith] that His divine providence and power extend to all groups and individuals.

Rabbi Moshe Cordovero's writings also may contain the same internal contradictions. We have quoted Rabbi Cordovero's *Shiur Komah* often, as it eloquently presents the traditional view of divine providence. However, in his more studied *Tomer Devorah* he intimates that specific individual divine providence extends beyond human beings:

Furthermore, it is the nature of Wisdom to provide for all that exists, for it is the thought which contemplates all creatures... Furthermore, His mercy extend to all creatures, neither destroying nor despising any of them. For the Supernal Wisdom is extended to all created things: minerals, plants, animals, and humans...

4. Additionally, it may be that some of the sources do disagree, but others do not.

through specific individual divine providence means to experience that providence on a level that is recognizable. When this reality cannot be sensed, it appears that the person, animal, plant, etc. is governed by chance and nature. But in truth they are not. The specific individual attention that governs this person, animal, plant, or inanimate object is equally providential to that which governs the most pious and righteous individual, but it takes a hidden form.

Accordingly, the Ramban's statement (Genesis 18:19) that except for the completely righteous, man is "left to the influence of chance" is understood as follows: When man is left to chance, he doesn't lose specific individual divine providence in reality. He merely looses overt providence. The way things occur do not seem to have a method; they appear as chance. Instead of overt specific individual divine providence, he is governed by hidden specific individual divine providence — but specific individual divine providence nonetheless.

This may be the proper explanation of the following comments of the Ramban in Deuteronomy 11:13, which we discussed in chapter three:

> You should know that [overt] miracles are not performed, whether for good or bad, except for the completely righteous or completely evil individuals. However regarding regular people, the way of the world (*minhago shel olam*) orchestrates for them good and bad, according to their actions.

The last phrase, "according to their actions," makes it clear that even though *minhago shel olam* is governing them, it isn't a completely haphazard system. The governance of nature is still a form, albeit it a more hidden form, of specific individual divine providence that governs "according to their actions."

Ramban also states this quite clearly elsewhere in his commentary (Exodus 6:2):

> The rewards and punishments of the Torah in this world all take the form of hidden miracles — they appear to the casual ob-

server as following the natural way of the world, but really they are reward and punishment.

Rabbi Meir Leibush, the Malbim, also makes the observation that *mikreh*, chance, is a form of divine providence. In the book of Ruth (2:3), the verse reads, "She set out and came and gleaned in the field after the reapers, and she happened to come (*va-yikar mikreh*) to the field belonging to Boaz, who was a member of Elimelech's family." The Malbim comments that this supposed "*mikreh*" was divine providence, and cites other examples of divine providence referred to as *mikreh*.

In addition to the term *mikreh*, hidden forms of specific individual divine providence are also referred to as *teva*, nature. But, in truth, there is nothing natural about it. It is complete specific individual divine providence, every event and happening governed directly by God. This hidden form of God's governance is referred to as "nature" only because it is imperceptible and appears to lack design.

The Vilna Gaon's comments discussed above in chapter 4 allude to this understanding (*Yahel Ohr, Shelach* 157b):

> Even the way of nature (*hanhagas ha-teva*) is directly controlled by God's judgment and divine providence. "For man does not jam his finger below, unless it was so decreed in heaven" (*Chulin* 7b), and even a bird is not trapped without a decree from above. However nature is the messenger [of this heavenly decree].

Commenting on this statement, the author of Sefer *Emunah ve-Hashgachah*, written by a student of the Vilna Gaon, remarks (chapter 8): "This is always the way of nature — that one cannot detect the presence of divine providence [even though it is present]."

When Jewish thinkers say that certain humans, animals, plants, and inanimate objects are not under the governance of specific individual divine providence, they are only speaking in terms of man's perspective. However, in reality, these creatures are also governed by specific individual divine providence, albeit in a concealed form.

STAGE II:
REWARD AND PUNISHMENT

The fact that specific individual divine providence assumes an overt form in relation to humans and a hidden form in relation to non-humans suggests that the specific individual divine providence that governs humans stems from a different source, or at least operates differently, than that which governs non-humans.

Specific individual divine providence for humans operates through a system of reward and punishment. God governs human beings according to the merit of their actions and the depth of their beliefs, bestowing reward or punishment in response to their deeds.

Specific individual divine providence for non-humans does not emanate from a system of reward and punishment. This is because animals, plants, and other inanimate objects are irrelevant to such a system.[5] Hence, even though God does directly orchestrate the events of their lives, this orchestration is not in response to their actions. To illustrate, God does directly decide which leaf will fall off of a tree, but not because the leaf deserves to fall off the tree, or because the leaf needs to be punished.

Accordingly, we appreciate the many references to the system of reward and punishment found in the previously quoted discussions of divine providence. For instance, we discussed the Radak's remarks in his commentary on the book of Jonah (1:2):

> There is great confusion among the scholarly, for some contend that when a lion tears a lamb asunder, or a similar occurrence, it is a *punishment* for the [lamb] from God ...There are others who contend that there is not *reward and punishment* except for the human species alone.

---

5. Rabbi Luzzato writes in *Ma'amar ha-Ikarim* (*be-gemul*): "Man has an additional quality that does not exist with any other species...[namely,] that his deeds are recompensed measure for measure."

Rabbi Yosef Ergas implicitly states the connection between overt specific individual divine providence and the system of reward and punishment, in the following except from our earlier discussion:

> The first form of divine providence is a general form of providence for all created species in this world *that aren't destined for [divine] justice*...there is no need for the individuals to have [specific individual] divine providence.[6]

The same is true regarding an earlier quote from Rabbi Luzzato in *Ma'amar ha-Ikarim*, where he also makes a direct reference to reward and punishment in his discussion of specific individual divine providence:

> God constantly oversees all things that He created, and He sustains and directs each entity according to the purpose for which it was created. Since man is unique in that *he is rewarded and punished for his deeds*, as discussed earlier, the providence that applies to him must be different from that over all other species.

We can also look to our much-analyzed comments of the Ramban in his famous discussion in Exodus 13:16, where he also links divine providence with the system of reward and punishment.

> There were also those who admitted to God's knowledge, but denied divine providence, thus equating man with the fish of the sea — who are not governed [with divine providence], *and have no system of reward and punishment.* Such people say: "God has forsaken the world" (Ezekiel 9:9).

Our approach is also consistent with the Rambam's prolific statement in *Moreh Nevuchim*. Even though the Rambam writes clearly that specific individual divine providence does not apply to non-humans, it can be argued that he means to say that non-humans do not experience specific individual divine providence as a result of

---

6.   *Shomer Emunim haKadmon*, argument 2, section 81. See the full quote at the beginning of this chapter.

the system of reward and punishment. This reading of the Rambam emerges from a simple analysis of the Rambam's context in *Moreh Nevuchim*. In presenting his personal understanding of divine providence, the Rambam is directly responding to the view of the Muslim Mu'tazilite philosophers, who argue that a system of reward and punishment governs all of creation, even non-humans. This approach is illogical and flawed, according to the Rambam, and it is in reference to their erroneous view that the Rambam makes his statement and contends that only humans experience reward and punishment.

> I believe that divine providence in this lower world, that is under the lunar spheres, is directed towards the human species alone. Only [the human] species [is governed with divine providence] — in every detail [of life], and all good and bad that occurs to him — *in accordance with what he deserves.*

The Rambam is not necessarily denying that non-humans experience specific individual divine providence; he is merely arguing that they do not receive it as part of the system of reward and punishment.

According to this understanding we can also better appreciate an enigmatic expression of the Ramban in his comments to Genesis 18:19, that "also humans are left to the influence of chance, until their appointed time arrives" (discussed in chapter 3). What is this "appointed time" and why at that point are certain humans no longer left to the influence of chance?

According to our current understanding, the Ramban is stating that certain humans are denied the level of specific individual divine providence that is a product of reward and punishment, until the time of their death. For when a man passes away, i.e., "his appointed time arrives," he is surely subject to reward and punishment, as all people are judged when their earthly existence comes to an end.

Stage III:
The Revelation of God's Glory

If non-humans are outside of a system of reward and punishment, why would they be governed by specific individual divine providence? For what purpose would God desire a specific leaf to fall off of a tree?[7]

Let's return to an earlier point that we introduced at the end of chapter 1 and further developed in chapters 2 and 3. We discussed the principle that even according to the traditional approach, non-human creations may experience specific individual divine providence, but not on account of themselves, rather on account of their impact or relationship to a human. From this perspective, even a leaf has the potential to be judged by God. God must assess the role that a specific leaf plays in the scheme of those humans who are governed with specific individual divine providence. If the falling of a leaf will impact the life of a human who receives specific individual divine providence, God decrees it through the conduit of specific individual divine providence. Not on account of this leaf as a leaf, but on account of the human who is affected by the falling of this leaf.

This perspective accounts for situations where the life of a human is affected by the fate of a non-human. Yet there are seemingly

---

7. One response could be that God's reasons are beyond human comprehension, and that such a question is futile and even reflects a sense of intellectual arrogance. However, the Ramban, in his monumental essay on theodicy, *Sha'ar ha-Gemul*, argues that this overly humble approach is not the way of the wise. The Ramban's context is a discussion of the presence of evil in a world created by God — Who is the source and embodiment of ultimate goodness. The Ramban lambastes those who maintain that because God's system of reward and punishment is beyond human comprehension, man should not attempt to understand it; he classifies such an approach as "the view of those who despise wisdom." The Ramban encourages the exertion of all of one's cerebral effort to intellectually grasp God's ways (with the realization that ultimately God's ways are beyond human understanding).

so many instances and events in the universe that do not directly impact humanity, and would not warrant the governance of specific individual divine providence on account of mankind. Does one leaf in a remote forest fall as a result of specific individual divine providence on account of mankind?

The answer of the Sanzer Rav is yes. In an attempt to justify the expansive view of divine providence in light of the Rambam's approach in *Moreh Nevuchim*, he writes (*Divrei Chayim, Miketz*):

> Granted that the Rambam has a different opinion regarding this, but in truth, according to our Sages, even a bird is not trapped without specific individual divine providence from Above (Yerushalmi, *Shvi'is*). Furthermore, it is known that all of creation is on account of man (*Zohar, Tazria* 48a) ... and even if we do not know how or why, [nevertheless] it is true, for there is nothing extra [or unnecessary] in creation, and that which appears extra is also for a specific purpose relating to mankind...[8]
>
> Man is governed with specific individual divine providence over all his limbs, needs, and [life] details, and thus all [of creation] receives [specific individual] divine providence on his account.

If this explanation was the only reason a leaf has specific individual divine providence, then our whole discussion here is merely a reformulation of the caveat and qualification presented at the end of chapter 1,[9] with the additional point that, in some esoteric way,

---

8. Rabbi Halberstam seemingly alludes here to the issues we raised regarding the sheer volume of "vessels" extrinsically receiving specific individual divine providence on account of the few individuals who intrinsically merit such governance.

9. Namely, when an animal, plant, or any created entity is owned by a person, or directly impacts the life of a person, the animal, plant, or created entity may experience specific individual divine providence. However this specific individual divine providence governs the animal, plant, or created entity, not on its own account or merit, but only on account of its impact and interaction with a human being. The divine providence is really just an extension of the divine providence of the human being.

everything that occurs in the life of non-humans makes an impact on humanity, and is therefore included within the caveat.

• • •

We will now suggest an additional approach to our issue, i.e., if non-humans are outside of the system of reward and punishment, why would they be governed by specific individual divine providence? This additional approach should not be viewed as an alternate approach,[10] rather it should be seen as a complementary perspective that enhances and magnifies our current understanding.

To properly grasp this second perspective, we must probe deeper into the foundations of God's governance. Rabbi Luzzato, in *Da'as Tevunos*, describes two concurrent systems of divine influence that operate in the world: *hanhagas ha-mishpat* and *hanhagas ha-yichud*. *Hanhagas ha-mishpat* is the system of reward and punishment that we are familiar with, where man is rewarded for his proper behavior and punished for his sins. However there is an additional system operating in the world. All that exists was created with the eventual goal of manifesting the glory of God in the world. As the verse states, "All was created for His glory" (*Avos* 6:11). This goal finds expression in the end of days when all people and creations will declare the glory of God. *Hanhagas ha-yichud* is the ever-unfolding process of the eventual divine manifestation. All creations and history are part of an evolutionary process that is building toward a revelation of God's glory, and this process operates concurrently in our world with the system of reward and punishment.[11]

Using this concept we can explain that the specific individual divine providence of human beings operates as part of *hanhagas*

---

10. That everything in creation, in some way, affects the lives of humans and hence experiences specific individual divine providence.

11. We should not make any erroneous deduction from this statement. The system of *hanhagas ha-mishpat* also ultimately leads to an eventual revelation of God's glory.

ha-mishpat, while all non-humans operate as part of *hanhagas ha-yichud*. Certainly the non-human creations are governed by specific individual divine providence, but it does not reflect or respond to their actions; rather, it acts upon them as is necessary for the process of the eventual revelation of God's glory.

To return to our question, the reason that specific individual divine providence governs non-humans, even though they are outside of the system of reward and punishment, is because the fate of every creature is necessary for the unfolding revelation of God's glory. Granted they do not require specific individual divine providence on account of *hanhagas ha-mishpat*, but on account of *hanhagas ha-yichud* they most certainly do.

If we return to one of our quotations of an advocate of the expansive view, we realize that he may have been alluding to this perspective. Rabbi Menachem Mendel of Vitebsk, in his work *Pri ha-Aretz* (*Bo*), wrote:

> It is hard for evil people [to believe] and their hearts reject [the belief in] specific individual divine providence — that no person stubs his toe, and no blade of grass dries out and is uprooted, and no rock is strewn about, unless it is the destined time and place for such an event to occur... All is from God, and serves to reveal His Godliness, wisdom, and attributes...

Rabbi Menachem Mendel of Vitebsk was in fact stating the expansive view that all things, even non-human entities, receive specific individual divine providence. However the context of that specific individual divine providence is not necessarily reward and punishment, but rather to reveal divine Godliness and wisdom in the world.

With this, we gain a better understanding of the role of nature. God's governance through the system of *hanhagas ha-yichud* is called nature, *teva*. The kabbalistic masters[12] teach that the *gematria*

---

12. The Vilna Gaon quoted in Sefer *Emunah ve-Hashgachah* (chapter 8) and others.

(numerical value) of *teva* (nature) is the same as God's name, Elokim. This is because the system of nature is really just the unfolding process of God's eventual revelation in the world. We have quoted Rabbi Ergas as stating that the reality of all created things being governed directly by God is the secret of the numerical value of Elokim equaling *teva*. This cryptic statement is now more clearly understood. The system of nature, *teva*, is really the mask that hides an unfolding Godly process of divine revelation.

We are now presented with a further understanding of the Ramban's concept of being "left to the influence of chance." When an individual is righteous and dedicated to the goals of mankind, he is governed by specific individual divine providence through the process of *hanhagas ha-mishpat*. But, when an individual is distracted from God, and divorces himself from his divine mission, he is "left to the influence of chance" — meaning, he is no longer judged based on his merit, and is not dealt within the arena of *hanhagas ha-mishpat*. Instead, he is relegated to the level of the rest of creation and judged only by his role in the universe's evolution towards the revelation of God's glory, *hanhagas ha-yichud*. Since his actions and initiatives do not determine his fate, rather dependent on other factors, he is classified as being "left to the influence of chance."

Indeed, the Ohr ha-Chayim defines being "left to the influence of chance" as an existence outside the system of reward and punishment. God states in the Torah, "And if you walk with me *keri*, and will not hearken unto Me... Then will I also walk with you *be-keri*..." (Leviticus 26:21, 26). The Ohr ha-Chayim explains that this verse means that when individuals act properly and merit specific individual divine providence, then they are treated according to their actions, i.e., reward and punishment. But if they act *be-keri*, meaning they fail to take the message of punishment, and instead attribute everything to chance and not to divine providence, so then God will treat them through the medium of chance. Meaning, they will receive punishments and rewards that are not necessarily appropriate for their deeds or conducive to enabling their repentance.

In effect, the Ohr ha-Chayim is saying that when individuals are "left to the influence of chance" they still receive providence directly from God, but it is not meted out based on a system of reward and punishment.

• • •

And with this we return to the goal of mankind. If an individual realizes the specific individual divine providence that governs his existence, and seeks to internalize this reality, he will then be elevated and dealt with according to his actions. However when a person ascribes his daily occurrences to chance and happenstance, so then God no longer governs him based on his actions. Granted God watches over him providentially, and even with specific individual divine providence, but the divine providence doesn't operate through a system of reward and punishment. He can receive punishments that are not appropriate for his actions and is seemingly exposed to the influence of chance and happenstance.

PART TWO

SPECIFIC INDIVIDUAL DIVINE PROVIDENCE

AND

FREE WILL

PART TWO
INTRODUCTION

U ntil now we have focused on the specific individual divine providence that governs humanity. We have assumed that whenever events occur in the life of a God-fearing person, the sole source is God's decree. However, when we probe deeper into the issues involved, a difficulty arises.

The concept of an individual's free will is one of the central principles of the Jewish faith. In Deuteronomy (30:19) God declares, "I call heaven and earth to witness against you this day, that I have set before you life and death, blessing and curse; therefore choose life, so that you may live, you and your offspring."

The Rambam, in the eighth chapter of *Shemoneh Perakim*, affirms this fundamental principle and ascribes to it the Talmudic maxim, "All is in the hands of Heaven except for the fear of Heaven" (*Berachos* 33b, *Megilah* 25a, and *Nidah* 16b).

The actions of man are given over to him. No one forces him regarding them, and no one, except for himself, leads him towards an elevated existence or a lowly existence... If man was forced regarding his actions, all of the Torah's positive and negative commandments would be irrelevant...so, too, reward and punishment would be a complete injustice...

The undeniable truth is that man's actions are given over to him. If he wants he can act, and if he does not want to, he does not have to. There is nothing forcing him whatsoever. And that which we find [in the sayings of] our Sages, "All is in the hands of Heaven, except for the fear of Heaven," is also true and addresses that which we have discussed. The positive and negative commandments of the Torah are there for man to do or not to do. Through these [commandments] man will acquire the fear of Heaven — and this [decision to fulfill the commandments] is not in the hands of Heaven, but rather given over to man's free will, as we explained. If so what is the meaning of "All is in the hands of Heaven"? This refers to natural things regarding which man has no choice, such as if he is tall or short.

If humanity is endowed with free will, how can specific individual divine providence govern all things that occur? Granted, if an animal attacks a person, or a river floods and destroys property, we can avow that God's specific individual divine providence was responsible, for neither the animal nor the river possess free will. However when an individual, endowed with free will, decides to act, to what extent is specific individual divine providence the operative force? Since an individual has free reign to act as he desires, can we still maintain that when he decides to strike another individual, the victim was harmed because of specific individual divine providence? Did a divine decree orchestrate this assault, or was it merely the result of the perpetrator's divinely granted free will?

Part Two of this book addresses this complex issue. The first two chapters present the traditional approach of Jewish thinkers; the third chapter presents a restrictive approach argued by a minority of Jewish thinkers; and the final chapter, developing themes from Part One, suggests a philosophic construct for bridging these seemingly disparate approaches.

CHAPTER 1
THE TRADITIONAL APPROACH

The traditional approach contends that man's free will does not function independently of divine providence. In other words, an individual's action against his fellow is only realized if the intended result fulfills a divine decree. If there is no divine decree against the intended recipient, even an individual possessing free will is powerless against him.

Rabbi Bachya ben Yosef ibn Paquda[1] in his monumental work of Jewish thought, *Chovos ha-Levavos* (*Sha'ar ha-Bitachon*, chapter 3), articulates this understanding.

> No creation has the ability to bring benefit or harm to himself or another without the acquiescence of God. [It is crucial that one realize this, because] when a slave has more than one master, and all of them are able to bring him benefit, he is unable to rely on only one of them, because he hopes for assistance from all

---

1.   Spain, d. 11th century.

of them. And if one of them has the ability to bring him more benefit than the others, he will rely more on that master — to a degree commensurate with that master's ability [to bring the slave benefit] — but he will still retain a degree of reliance on the other masters. However, if only one [of the masters] is able to bring him benefit or harm, he will naturally rely on that one master alone, for he does not anticipate assistance from the others. When a person has internalized that no creation can bring him benefit or harm except with God's acquiescence, he will stop fearing others and relying upon them. [He] will rely only on God alone, as the verse in Psalms states: "Do not place your trust in princes, nor in human beings, in whom there is no help."

In an attempt to demonstrate the extent of God's providence within the traditional approach, Rabbi Yisrael Zamosc[2] relates the following parable in his *Tov ha-Levanon*, a popular commentary on *Chovos ha-Levavos*:

A ship filled with sea-bound individuals was set to sail on the morrow. However, the town governor issued a fallacious accusation against the ship captain, delaying the intended departure. During the delay, a naval war erupted in the very sea the ship had intended to cross. Fearing the crossfire, the crew decided to take a different route to avoid the war. However, the new route had unknown treacherous conditions, and the ship struck a rock and sunk, killing all those aboard. When the ship capsized, a chest filled with treasures was lifted by the waves and carried toward shore. At just that time, the local governor of the area close to where the ship sank accused a local citizen of a crime, and the accused individual fled for his life toward the shore. When he reached the water, the treasure-laden chest was, at that moment, washed ashore, and the accused individual lived the rest of his life off of the treasures he found in the chest.

After listing the many occurrences that had to transpire for the original false accusation of the ship captain to eventually lead to the later individual's new-found wealth, Rabbi Yisrael Zamosc concludes that everything that occurred in this tale — the false accusations, the war, the capsized ship, etc. — was decreed by God, and attests to the complexity and extent of divine providence. In His infinite wisdom, God is able to ensure specific individual divine providence for one individual, without compromising the free will of any other individual.

Rabbi Avraham Maimonides,[3] son of the Rambam, also espouses this view in his commentary on the Torah, commenting on the verse, "And if a man does not act intentionally, but God causes it to come to hand, then I will appoint you a place to where you may flee" (Exodus 21:13).

> A truth of our faith is that any individual who dies, via any cause, does so ultimately on account of a divine decree. And hence, one who is killed by a willful murderer [dies on account] of God's decree that he should die through the medium of murder. [However, God] did not force the murderer to kill this individual, and for this reason [the murderer] is deserving of punishment.

In *Sefer Chasidim* (sect. 751), attributed to Rabbi Yehudah Ha-Chasid,[4] the traditional view is also expressed:

> If any individual falls ill, he should not ascribe this sickness to any food or drink, and thus assume it is not from God. And even if evil men beat him [he should ascribe it only to God, and] say that his sins caused it to occur. As the verse states, "For I set all men [against each other], each individual against his fellow" (Zachariah 8:10). And as it is written, "Shall evil befall a city, and God not be responsible?" (Amos 3:6). Rather [God] is definitely responsible. Furthermore, it states, "What is this that God has done to us?" (Genesis 42:28).[5] Therefore, it behooves man

---

3.   Egypt, d. 1237.
4.   Germany, d. 1217.
5.   In the Chida's (Rabbi Chayim Yosef Dovid Azuli, Jerusalem-Italy, d. 1806)

to pray regarding all types of things that befall him — whether through [the hands of] man or [the hands of] Heaven.

This approach was also adopted by many later-day thinkers as well. In the letters of Rabbi Yosef Zundel of Salant,[6] the traditional approach is ascribed to Rabbi Eliyahu of Vilna, the Vilna Gaon.

> The brilliant rabbi, teacher of the entire exile, our master, Rabbi Chayim of Volozhin, said: I heard from the pious one [i.e., the Gaon of Vilna], may his memory be blessed, and I as well have maintained since my youth, that there is an error which the masses believe — and even the Rambam concurs with this [erroneous] view — that a free-willed creature is able to affect an individual without a divine decree. Rather [the truth is] that all things that occur to an individual are decreed, [even] which rock will strike him. However, when it comes to a free-willed creature it is not decreed which [specific] free-willed creature will do him good or bad [only that which will transpire is decreed]. And if there is no decree from Heaven [whatsoever, not even] a free-willed creature is able to affect him in any way.

This view was also endorsed by leading Chasidic scholars. For instance, Rabbi Shneur Zalman of Liadi,[7] the founder of Chabad Chasidism, adopts the traditional approach in the *Igeres ha-Kodesh* section of his work on Chasidic thought, *Tanya*.

Our Sages teach, "One who gets angry is likened to an idol wor-

---

commentary on *Sefer Chasidim*, titled *Bris Olam*, he explains that when the prophet Amos proclaims that all evil that occurs in the city is from God, it apparently includes even evil that is brought about through the hands of free-willed humans. The Chida also notes that when the brothers of Joseph lament the fact that their money was found in their sacks after they departed Egypt, and they fear the wrath of the viceroy of Egypt, they proclaim in despair, "What is this that God has done to us?" even though the money was undoubtedly placed in their sacks by humans.

6. Lithuania-Israel, d. 1866. The letter under discussion is found in *Kisvei Rebbi Yosef Zundel me-Salant* in the section entitled "Questions, Stories, and Practices from Rabbi Eliyahu of Vilna and Rabbi Chayim of Volozhin."

7. Russia, d. 1812.

shipper." The reason for this equation is clear to those who possess understanding: at the time of one's anger, faith in God disappears. For had he believed that "This is God's doing" (Psalms 118:23) he would not have been angered at all. And even though a human being, who is a free-willed creature, cursed him, or hit him, or damaged his property, and is therefore guilty in terms of human courts and divine punishment (on account of his bad decisions), nevertheless [one should realize] that regarding the victim [i.e., he himself], such occurrences reflect God's decree, and God has many able messengers.

Even into the modern era the traditional approach has been continually favored by the greatest Jewish thinkers, as the following excerpt from the writings of the Chafetz Chayim attests (*Shem Olam*, chapter 3, footnote):

All forms of suffering that occur to an individual — when someone insults him or abuses him — are from God, and on account of his sins... If an individual strikes another person, even willfully, this too is divine providence from Above... A proof for this fact is found in the Torah (Exodus 21:18–19): "If two men fight, and one smites...he shall only pay for the loss of time [from work], and [the victim] shall be thoroughly healed." Our Sages teach [regarding this verse], "From here we learn permission for doctors to heal, and that one should not say, 'God inflicted, and He will heal.' " Behold this verse addresses a situation when one individual willfully smites another during a fight [and yet, it is referred to by the Sages as "God inflicted"]! Perforce, one sees that [suffering inflicted by another individual] is in the hands of God.

THE CULPABILITY PARADOX

According to the traditional approach — that all occurrences, even those perpetrated by individuals possessing free will, are governed completely by divine providence — the culpability of the perpetrating free-willed individual demands investigation. If all happenings that affect an individual are governed, and even decreed, by God, can the "messenger" of these occurrences be held accountable? Is such an individual not carrying out the pre-decreed mission of God?

As to be expected, this weighty issue was addressed by many thinkers who espoused the traditional approach. Rabbi Sa'adiah Gaon,[8] in *Emunos ve-Deos* (4:5) confronts this perplexity:

> People ask: Is the murder of an individual to be ascribed to God? ... What can one say regarding such an event, and to whom can we ascribe [the killing]?
>
> We maintain that the death of an individual is an act of God, but the [element of] murder is the act of the wicked. Since God decreed death [for this individual], had the murderer not acted willfully and killed him, [the victim] would surely have died in another way.[9] And the same is true regarding a thief: if we view an individual's partial monetary loss as a punishment or a test, how do we classify the act of stealing? Is it considered an act of God? The proper response is that the fact the item was lost was indeed an act of God, but the fact it was stolen was an act of man. For since God decreed that the item should be lost, had the thief not stolen the item, it would have been lost in another way. Such was the response of Shemayah and his brother to one of the Roman kings, when they said, "We have been sentenced to death by Heaven. If you do not kill us, God has many executioners at His disposal to strike us" (*Ta'anis* 18b).

Rabbi Sa'adiah Gaon maintains the traditional approach, that an individual could not possibly be murdered if God did not decree his impending death. However, such a decree, Rabbi Sa'adiah argues,

---

8.   Babylonia, d. 942.

9.   Note that according to Rabbi Sa'adiah the victim was destined for death, but not necessarily murder. However, according to Rabbi Avraham Maimonides, quoted above, the victim was destined specifically to be murdered.

does not provide another individual carte blanche to perpetrate a murder. As an individual possessing free will, the murderer exercises his prerogative to carry out a horrific act, and will be punished accordingly. But the fact the victim died as a result of this murderer's actions — the success of the act — lies in the domain of God's governance. Had the murdered not acted, the victim would have surely died through other means. According to Rabbi Sa'adiah's presentation, an individual possessing free will is held completely responsible for his actions, even though the results would have occurred anyway.

This paradoxical[10] approach, asserting both a perpetrator's culpability and a victim's invincibility to non-divinely ordained occurrences, appears in the writings of many other thinkers. The above-quoted Torah commentary of Rabbi Avraham Maimonides states this explicitly:

One who is killed by a willful murderer [dies on account] of God's decree that he should die through the medium of murder. [However, God] did not force the murderer to kill this individual, *and for this reason [the murderer] is deserving of punishment.*

Additionally, the aforementioned epistle of Rabbi Shneor Zalman of Liadi eludes to this paradox:

And even though a human being, who is a free-willed creature, cursed him, or hit him, or damaged his property, *and is therefore guilty, in terms of human courts and divine punishment, on account of his bad decisions...*

A vital linchpin in maintaining this paradoxical position is the Talmud's discussion in *Ta'anis* 18b. The Talmud relates:

When Turyanus sought to kill Lulianus and his brother, Pappus, in Ludkia, he said to them: "If you are from the nation

---

10. Note the difference between a paradox and a contradiction. While a contradiction contains an internal conflict or inconsistency, a paradox merely appears to be a contradiction, but in truth contains no internal conflict.

of Chananyah, Mishael, and Azaryah, let your God come and save you from my hand, similar to the way he saved Chananyah, Mishael, and Azaryah from the hand of Nevuchadnezer." They replied to him: "Chananyah, Mishael, and Azaryah were completely righteous men and thus deserved that a miracle occur on their behalf. [Furthermore] Nevuchadnezer was a proper king and thus deserved that a miracle occur through him. But you [lit. that evil one] are a fool and thus not deserving that a miracle occur through [you]. We have been sentenced to death by Heaven, and if you do not kill us, God has many executioners at His disposal, and God has many bears and lions in His world that can attack and kill us. But God only placed us into your hands in order to punish you on account of our blood on your hands..."

As Rabbi Sa'adiah Gaon explained, the resolution of the paradox of human culpability and divine decrees begins with the statement of Lulianus and Pappus that "God has many executioners at his disposal, and God has many bears and lions in His world that can attack and kill us." The death of Lulianus and Pappus was divinely decreed, and would occur whether Turyanus executed them or not, for God has many viable messengers with which to realize His desires. This fact notwithstanding, Turyanus' free-willed decision to be the vessel through which the divine decree would be realized justifies his culpability and consequential punishment for the murders.[11]

---

11. Rabbi Eliyahu Eliezer Dessler develops the principle that God is not bound by time, and that the past, present, and future is all one to God. Time is a this-world creation, and does not exist from God's perspective. Due to this fact, God, in His infinite wisdom, is aware of the evil choices man will make when exercising free will. (This knowledge of man's future choices does not force man to make particular choices, since God's knowledge functions differently than human knowledge.) He is therefore able to arrange for human "vessels" to realize His divine decrees without compromising their free will. By knowing, and then utilizing, the evil choices humans will make, God always has at His disposal countless possible "vessels" to fulfill the necessary decrees on humanity.

• • •

To restate the principle ascribed to Rabbi Sa'adiah Gaon, based on the Talmudic dictum, "There are many messengers available for God's purposes," and developed in this chapter: God decrees all events that transpire, however, the emissary of the decree is not divinely ordained. When an individual acts through his free will he is held accountable, receiving reward for good deeds and assuming culpability for evil actions. God truly has many messengers available for His purposes, and no individual is forced to assume the responsibility to carry out a divine decree.

CHAPTER 2
BIBLICAL
MANIFESTATIONS

Many Jewish thinkers focus on specific events in biblical history that highlight the paradox of balancing human culpability with the reality of divine providence. In this chapter we will explore some of those events, and the relevant discussions of Jewish thinkers. The goal of this analysis is not only to document biblical precedent for Rabbi Sa'adiah Gaon's approach, but also to deepen our understanding of the issues.

THE EGYPTIAN SERVITUDE

On a national level, perhaps the most overt manifestation of the paradox of human culpability and divine providence was the Egyptian nation's enslavement of the Israelites. God told Abraham in the "Covenant between the Parts" that the Israelites will be enslaved by the Egyptians for many years, and that God will then visit judgment upon the Egyptians and punish them for enslaving the Israelites. The culpability of the Egyptians for carrying out the divine promise to Abraham presents a theological difficulty.

At first glance, the approach of Rabbi Sa'adiah Gaon developed in the last chapter may not suffice for the issue of the Egyptian servitude. For in this case the "messenger of God" was identified. The decree was that the Egyptians specifically would enslave the Israelites. Hence, it seems hard to argue that the fact the Egyptians opted to carry out the decree is a reason to hold them accountable.

However, upon revisiting the verses in the "Covenant between the Parts" it is noted that the Torah does not single out, nor even mention, the Egyptians. In Genesis 15:13–14 the Torah merely states:

> Know for sure that your descendants will be strangers in a land not their own, and they will serve them, and they will cause them to suffer for four hundred years. And also the nation they serve, I will judge, and afterward they will come out with great possessions.

In these lines, the "land not their own" and the oppressing "they" are not identified. Thus, according to the approach of Rabbi Sa'adiah Gaon, the argument can be made that the Egyptians are culpable because they, with their own free will, chose to be the emissaries of God's oppressive decree against the Israelites.

The Rambam, however, assumes that the Egyptians *were* singled out to be the emissaries of God's decree, even though the verse does not mention them specifically. According to the Rambam's understanding, the culpability of the Egyptians requires an explanation.

To address this issue, the Rambam argues that even though the Egyptians, as a nation, were chosen by God to be the vehicle for oppressing the Jewish nation, each individual Egyptian citizen did not have to join the national movement. When each individual acted on his own free will and chose to assist in oppressing the Israelites, this act of human volition warranted and justified culpability and punishment. The Rambam writes (*Hilchos Teshuvah* 6:5):

> And behold it is written in the Torah, "They [the descendants of
> Abraham] will serve them, and they [the Egyptians] will cause
> them to suffer" (Genesis 15:13–14). Behold [God] decreed upon
> the Egyptians to perpetrate evil. So, too, it is written, "And this
> people [the Israelites] will rise up, and go astray after the foreign
> gods of the land." Behold [God] decreed upon the Israelites to
> engage in idolatry. And so, how can God punish them?...
>
> Each and every one of those Egyptians, and all those who did
> evil to the Israelites, had the ability to not bring evil upon the
> Israelites, if they so desired. For [God] did not decree on any
> specific individual [that they must oppress the Israelites], rather
> [God] only informed [Abraham] that eventually his descendants
> would be enslaved in a "land not their own."[1]

Similar to the Rambam's approach, one can also suggest that
the generation of Egyptians that chose to oppress the Israelites was
held culpable, because they, as a generation, did not need to be the
specific generation that fulfilled God's decree. Had they not acted
on their free will and oppressed the Israelites, a different generation
would have done so in their stead.

• • •

The Ra'avad, Rabbi Avraham ben Dovid of Posquieres,[2] in his
Hasagos, takes the Rambam to task for his aforementioned exposition,[3]

---

1. In the eighth chapter of the Rambam's *Shemoneh Perakim*, he explains
    similarly.
2. Provence, d. 1198.
3. The Ramban also criticizes the Rambam's approach (Ramban's Torah
    Commentary, Genesis 15:14):

    > The Rabbi [i.e., the Rambam] gave an explanation in his *Sefer ha-Madah*...
    > but his words are not correct in my opinion. Had [God] decreed that
    > one [non-specific] individual from all of the nations should mistreat [the
    > Israelites] in such-and-such a way, and one individual arose and fulfilled

and suggests an alternative explanation for Egyptian culpability.

The issue regarding the Egyptians is not a problem for two reasons…Had [the Egyptians] listened to Moses at the outset and freed Israel, they would not have been struck, nor drowned at sea. However, the brazenness of Pharaoh, and his disparagement of God before sending them, caused [their destruction].

Second, God said, "Cause them to suffer," and [the Egyptians] worked [the Israelites] exceedingly hard, and killed them, and drowned them. This is like the verse, "I was only a little angry, and they added to the evil" (Zachariah 1:15), and therefore [the Egyptians] are held accountable.

According to the Ra'avad, the Egyptians were not punished for the actual enslavement, for indeed it was divinely decreed that they would enslave the Israelites; rather, they were punished for acting beyond the limits of the divine decree. The Ra'avad first argues that had Pharaoh released the Israelites from bondage after Moses' first plea, the Egyptians would have been spared suffering and destruction. Second, the Ra'avad insists that God never decreed that the Egyptians should overwork the Israelites or throw the Israelite firstborns into the river. These actions went beyond the divine decree, and on account of these "extra" actions, the Egyptians were held responsible. According to both suggestions of the Ra'avad, the Egyptians were punished because they went beyond the bounds of the divine decree, either by enslaving the Israelites for too long, or in terms of the intensity of the enslavement.

---

the [non-specific] decree of God, [in my opinion] he would be deserving of merit [because he fulfilled God's desire]. How does [the Rambam] make any sense? If a king commands the people of a country to perform a particular act, one who is lazy and leaves the responsibility to another provokes [the king] to anger and forfeits his soul, while the one who carries out [the king's request] obtains favor from him. Moreover, the verse says "and also the nation whom they shall serve" — implying that [the Israelites] would serve the entire [Egyptian] nation. And [additionally we should note that the Israelites] went on their own to Egypt [hence, giving the Egyptians little choice in the matter].

The Ramban argues a similar approach in his commentary on the Torah. Commenting on the Torah's use of the phrase "And also" in the verse, "And also the nation they serve, I will judge..." (Genesis 15:14), the Ramban writes:

> The best explanation in my opinion is that the words "And also" are to be explained as follows: Even though I decreed on your descendants that they will be "strangers in a land that is not theirs," and will "serve them, and they will cause them to suffer," nonetheless I will judge the nation that they serve, on account of what [the Egyptians] will do to them. They will not be spared simply because they were fulfilling my divine decree. The reason for this [culpability] is described in the verse: "I have become zealous with a great zeal for Jerusalem and for Zion. I will become enraged with a great anger against the complacent nations, who added to the evil, when I was only slightly angry" (Zachariah 1:14–15). And similarly with Egypt, they increased the oppression[4] when they threw [the Israelites'] sons into the river, and when they embittered their lives and sought to eradicate them completely. For this reason, "I will judge," I will bring them to judgment [to ascertain] if they did as the divine decree mandated, or if they increased the oppression [beyond the bounds of the divine decree].

---

4.   At a later point in his commentary on this verse, the Ramban proves that the Egyptians indeed went beyond the bounds of the divine decree.

> It is clear that the Egyptian's throwing of the Israelite firstborns into the river was not included in [God's decree of] "And they will serve them, and they will cause them to suffer," but was rather [an attempt to] decimate them completely. And so, too, that which [the Egyptians] said at first, "Let us deal wisely with them, lest they multiply," [and the consequential increase in workload] was not included in the [decreed] "servitude" and "suffering." [These examples are in addition to] the actual intensification of suffering [committed by the Egyptians, as attested to in the verse], "And they embittered their lives with exceedingly hard work," and this is the intention of the verse, "And [God] saw our suffering, our toil, and our oppression."

The approach of the Ra'avad and the Ramban begs a further question: How was it humanly possible for the Egyptians to persecute the Israelites beyond the divine decree? If everything that occurs to an individual is only on account of a divine decree, as the traditional approach maintains, how could the Egyptians' actions affect the Israelites, if the additional persecution was not included in the divine decree?

Perhaps we can suggest that the Ra'avad and the Ramban are of the opinion that the Egyptians specifically were divinely decreed to be the vessels through which the Israelites would be enslaved; however, that enslavement had specific parameters and limits. This does not mean that the Israelites were not deserving of, or destined for, additional suffering. Indeed they were. But this additional suffering was not included within the parameters of the enslavement that the Egyptians were decreed to actualize. When the Egyptians stepped beyond the bounds of their divinely decreed role, and dealt exceedingly harshly with the Israelites, their actions were effective only because there was also a divine decree for this additional suffering. The Egyptians were held culpable because causing this additional suffering was not their role — as dictated by the divine decree — and could have been achieved through the "many messengers at God's disposal."

● ● ●

The Ramban also suggests an additional understanding to explain the culpability of the Egyptians in light of the divine decree.

> You should know and understand: [concerning] a man who is written and inscribed on Rosh Hashanah to be killed, the bandits who actually kill him are not guiltless on account of the fact that they have fulfilled the divine decree. Rather, the evil one will die for his sins, and the murderer will be held accountable for the blood [of the victim]. But when the divine decree is issued by a prophet, the one who fulfills [the divine decree] is subject

to varying rules. For if one hears the [prophet's charge] and [acts out of a] desire to fulfill the divine decree, he bears no iniquity. On the contrary, he receives merit [for his actions]…However, if one did not hear the prophet's charge, and killed him [i.e., the object of the divine decree] out of hatred or to rob him, he is deserving of punishment, for he intended to sin, and it is thus a sin for him.

The Ramban suggests that the Egyptians should be held accountable because their intentions were solely to persecute the Israelites; they lacked the proper intentions of fulfilling the divine decree. In the end, the Ramban suggests that the Egyptians were undoubtedly accountable on two accounts: they persecuted the Israelites beyond the bounds of the divine decree, and their intentions were not to fulfill God's plan.

• • •

The underlying factor in all the above quoted approaches is that liability is a product of volition. In order for an individual to be held accountable, there must be an expression of free will. According to the Rambam, it was each individual Egyptian's personal decision to join the nation's enslavement of the Israelites that begot culpability. The Ramban and Ra'avad argue it was the Egyptian nation's willingness to persecute the Israelites beyond the bounds of the divine decree. And according to the Ramban's second suggestion, it was the ill intentions of the Egyptians that explains their guilt.

All of these Jewish thinkers agree that even the direst Jewish suffering was divinely decreed, and yet the Egyptians were held accountable because of acts of their own free will.

King David and Shimi ben Geira

In Samuel II, the prophet relates the tragic saga of Absalom's rebellious attempt to usurp the throne from his father, King David.

In response to the masses' initial support of Absalom, King David is forced into exile and encounters the sagacious Shimi ben Geira[5] in the Benjamite town of Bahurim. Shimi ben Geira, in a public display of treachery against the exiled king, approaches David cursing and pelting rocks at his entourage. With accusations of murder, marital impropriety,[6] and unjust seizure of Saul's throne, Shimi ben Geira's spectacle generates severe embarrassment for King David. In defense of the king, Abishai ben Zuriah offers to slay Shimi ben Geira for his affront to the throne. In a great display of humility and self-control, King David declares (Samuel II 16:10–11):

> What does it matter to me or to you, O sons of Zuriah? So he will curse, for God has said to him, "Curse David." So who can say to him, "Why have you done this?"…Here my own son, who has come from my innards, desires to kill me, so what not of this Benjamite? Leave him be and let him curse, for God has told him to do so.

Based on our presentation thus far, the analysis of this passage requires two independent inquires. The first regards the divine decree against King David, and his response to the events in light of this decree. The second is the culpability of Shimi for his disrespectful cursing spate against the King.

King David's response, "For God has said to him, 'Curse David' " is a strong affirmation of Rabbi Sa'adiah's approach that even though Shimi acted on his own free will to curse King David, the ultimate reason David suffered public shame lies in a divine decree against King David, and not in the actions of Shimi ben Geira. This fact notwithstanding, the culpability of Shimi ben Geira is notably ambiguous in King David's statement. According to Rabbi Sa'adiah's approach, should not Shimi ben Geira be held accountable for his free-willed decision to attack King David?

---

5. The Talmud in *Berachos* 8a describes Shimi's greatness.

6. Abarbanel explains the different statements of Shimi as referring to the deaths of Abner, Ishboshes, and Uriah, and alluding to King David's retaining Batsheva as his wife.

Perhaps King David reasoned that Shimi ben Geira was completely guiltless for his action in this specific case. In verse 10, Rashi (s.v. *Hashem amar lo*) explains David's calculation: "Is it possible that a man like [Shimi], who is the head of the Sanhedrin, would curse the king if God didn't tell him to?"

According to Rashi's suggestion that King David realized that God indeed instructed Shimi ben Geira to curse him, we can invoke the Ramban's second approach outlined earlier in this chapter to completely absolve Shimi ben Geira of culpability. The Ramban stated above:

> …When the divine decree is issued by a prophet, the one who fulfills [the divine decree] is subject to varying rules. For if one hears the [prophet's charge] and [acts out of a] desire to fulfill the divine decree, he bears no iniquity. On the contrary, he receives merit [for his actions]…

Accordingly, Rashi may be suggesting that Shimi ben Geira's actions were not driven by a personal vendetta against the king. Rather, Shimi, a righteous sage and head of the Sanhedrin, was cursing David to fulfill a direct decree from God.

In truth though, this conclusion is not forthcoming from the text itself. Later in Kings I (2:8–9) David, on his deathbed, instructs his son Solomon to execute Shimi ben Geira for his rebellious behavior against the throne.

> And, behold, there is with you Shimi ben Geira, the Benjamite of Bahurim, who cursed me with a grievous curse on the day that I went to Machanaim. He came down to meet me at the Jordan, and I swore to him by God, saying: "I will not put you to death with the sword." But now, do not treat him as guiltless, for you are a wise man, and you will know what should be done to him, and you should bring his gray head down to the grave in blood.

This condemnation of Shimi ben Geira reflects his culpability for shaming David, and hence his guilt as one who acts treacherously against the king.

Irrespective of Shimi ben Geira's eventual culpability, the immediate response of King David, recorded in Samuel II, is an affirmation of Rabbi Sa'adiah's approach — for even though Shimi ben Geira was ultimately punished for his act of free will, David still attributed the shame he experienced to his own sins, and not to Shimi ben Geira.

• • •

The confrontation between David and Shimi ben Geira also provides a valuable lesson and perspective on human relations. The *Sefer ha-Chinuch* remarks in its discussion of the commandment to refrain from exacting revenge on one's fellowman (commandment 241):

> One of the roots of the commandment[7] is that man should know and internalize that all that happens to him, whether for good or bad, is on account of God. [Whether it occurs through] man, or through his kinsman, nothing occurs without it being the will of God. And so, when another individual causes him suffering or pain, he should know in his soul that his sins caused it, and [therefore] God decreed it upon him. [Thus,] he should not set his thoughts to exact revenge from him, for [the perpetrator] is not the [real] reason for the bad [that befell him], rather [his] sin is the [real] reason, as David, of blessed memory, stated, "Leave him be and let him curse, for God has told him to do so" (Samuel II 16:11). [David] attributed the matter to his sins, and not to Shimi ben Geira.

---

7. It should be noted that *Sefer ha-Chinuch* always provides a reason for the commandment under discussion. At times the Chinuch writes, "The root of the commandment is..." and in other instances he says, "One of the roots of the commandment is..." The issue requires further research, but perhaps the later construction is an admission to more than one possible reason, a theme found in the writings of many Rishonim (see responsa of Rabbi Solomon ben Aderes I:94, for example). Alternatively, the later construction may represent an uncertainty by the author.

The proper appreciation of the system of divine providence generates a healthy approach to exonerating those who wrong us, advising one to direct the accusatory finger inward, rather than at the messenger of the divine decree.

Armed with an internalized understanding of God's divine decrees, introspection becomes the operative response to tragedy, even when the hardship is realized through the hands of another. The *Sefer ha-Chinuch* encourages one to internalize that the vehicle for God's decree will surely be punished for his free-willed decision to harm, but the ultimate reason the perpetrator's attempts were realized was because of one's own sins and a consequential divine decree.

The same valuable lesson is borne out from an earlier event in biblical history. When Joseph, viceroy of Egypt, finally revealed himself to his brothers, the Torah relates, "And the brothers could not answer him, for they were afraid in his presence" (Genesis 45:3). To allay their fears, Joseph assures them (Genesis 45:5–8):

> Do not be grieved, nor angry with yourselves, that you sold me here; for God sent me before you to preserve life. For these two years there has been famine in the land; and there are still five more years in which there will be neither plowing nor harvest... So now it was not you that sent me here, but rather it was God...

Like King David after him, Joseph assures the brothers that from his perspective the brothers are not guilty for the vicissitudes of his life. "It was not you who sent me here," Joseph declares, for ultimately it was God's decree that accounts for the travails he experienced.[8]

---

8. We can suggest that viewing Joseph's behavior in this light helps us appreciate the depth of a midrashic statement in *Sifrei de-Agadata al Ester* (*Midrash Panim Acherim* 2:6). The Midrash teaches that when Shimi ben Geira came before David to apologize for his actions, he invoked the memory of Joseph because of Joseph's pious response to the brothers.

    "Behold, I come this day, the first of all the house of Joseph, to go down

Following the example set by Joseph and David, the *Sefer Chasidim* encourages a perspective similar to that of the *Sefer ha-Chinuch*. In section 183 the *Sefer Chasidim* relates the following anecdote, containing implicit advice:

> It happened that a particular individual caused a rabbi a great deal of grief. The members of the congregation said to the rabbi, "What a terrible sin this man is committing, tormenting you for no reason at all."
>
> "I don't blame this individual," the rabbi replied. "It is my own sins that have caused this."
>
> "But, Rabbi," the members responded, "you really should punish and curse him."
>
> "If I did that," the rabbi said, "I would be punishing and cursing myself, because my sins are the cause of all this trouble."
>
> It was in this spirit that when Shimi [ben Geira] cursed David, he responded, "Leave him be and let him curse, for God has told him to do so" (Samuel II 16:11). David thus implied, "My sin caused this to happen..."

• • •

Like the Egyptian servitude, the ordeal of Shimi ben Geira and David also illustrates the paradox of divine decrees and human culpability. Furthermore, and perhaps more importantly, it instructs one how to properly address hardship experienced through the hands of another.

---

to meet my lord the king" (Samuel II 19:21). But he was from [the tribe of] Benjamin, so why did he say from Joseph? Because with Joseph, his brothers brought evil upon him, but he brought upon them good, as it says, "Now therefore you should not fear; I will sustain you, and your little children, etc." (Genesis 50:21). Therefore, [Shimi ben Geira] said "the first of all the house of Joseph."

CHAPTER 3
THE RESTRICTIVE APPROACH

The traditional view that we have discussed until now is reflected in many sources and represents the view of many Jewish thinkers.[1] Yet there are other sources and thinkers that argue that a free-willed individual can affect other individuals even in the absence of a divine decree. The most famous formulation of this approach is found in the *Ohr ha-Chayim* Torah commentary of Rabbi Chayim ben Moshe Attar.[2]

The *Ohr ha-Chayim* comments on the following incident: Jacob had sent his son Joseph to visit his brothers in Shechem. Upon seeing him approach, the brothers, upset over his grandiose dreams

---

1. The list of thinkers who endorse the traditional view includes, but is not limited to, the Rambam, Rabbi Sa'adiah Gaon, the Ramban (to be discussed in this chapter), the Chinuch, Rabbeinu Bachaya ibn Paquda, Rabbi Avraham Maimonides, Rabbi Yehudah ha-Chasid, Rabbi Eliyahu of Vilna, and Rabbi Shneor Zalman of Liadi.

2. Morocco, d. 1743.

of dominion over them, decide to make an attempt on his life. In justification they exclaim, "Then we shall see what will become of his dreams" (Genesis 37:20). With the goal of saving Joseph's life, Reuben suggests that instead of slaying Joseph, it would be wiser to throw him into a large pit. Explaining how this course of action would save Joseph from death, the *Ohr ha-Chayim* comments (Genesis 37:21):

> For man possesses free will, and can [even] kill one who is not deserving of death, as opposed to wild animals which cannot harm man if he is not [already] condemned to death from Heaven. [I.e., if there was no divine decree of his death, the snakes and scorpions could not kill him.] This is what [the Torah] means, "[And Reuben heard their plan] and saved [Joseph] from their hands," meaning, from the hands of individuals invested with free will. With this [understanding], the brothers statement "we shall see what will become of his dreams" is undermined, because free will can oppose [a divine decree], and hence the fact that [they succeeded] in killing him would not be a proof that [Joseph] spoke falsely [when he said he would rule over them].

The brothers were interested in determining the veracity of Joseph's dream, and they therefore figured that if his life was endangered and he died, it would be a sure sign that his wild dreams of grandeur were false. Yet they faced a dilemma, claims the *Ohr ha-Chayim*. If they, as free-willed individuals, would execute him, this would not be a true indication of the divine plan for Joseph, nor would it determine the veracity of his dreams, as their volitional actions as free-willed individuals have the ability to take effect even in the absence of a divine decree. And so, only by adopting Reuben's plan of leaving Joseph to the forces of nature — wild animals and the like — would the truth of Joseph's dreams be determined.[3]

---

3. Not everyone understands the *Ohr ha-Chayim* literally. For example, Rabbi Chayim Kanievsky, as recorded in Rabbi Tsvi Yavrov's *Derech Sichah* (*Miketz*), states that the *Ohr ha-Chayim* cannot be accepted on the literal level. Rather, the *Ohr ha-Chayim* was merely saying that more merits are

The *Ohr ha-Chayim* argues that free will trumps a divine decree, and hence the actions of a free-willed individual operate "outside" or "above" the realm of divine providence. Therefore, if Joseph were at the mercy of the brothers, they, as free-willed individuals, would have unrestricted power to harm or kill him, even if there was no divine decree to that effect.

Two centuries before Rabbi Chayim Attar's presentation of the more restrictive approach, Rabbi Moshe Alshich[4] had already eluded to the same theme in the Torah's portrayal of the brothers' attempt to kill Joseph. After reading the *Ohr ha-Chayim*'s longer explanation, Rabbi Alshich's terse references are understood to be predicated on this restrictive approach to divine providence (Genesis 37:21):

> [Reuben's] full intention was to save him from their hands — since they possess free will, and do not lack the ability to follow through on their plans.

Rabbi Naftali Zvi Yehudah Berlin, the Netziv,[5] in his *Harchev Davar* (Genesis 37:21), also presents the restrictive approach. The Netziv's comments are noteworthy in that he identifies the *Zohar* as the original source for the restrictive approach.[6]

---

necessary to save an individual from the hands of a free-willed person than are needed to save an individual from an animal. Indeed, many of the sources that will be discussed in this chapter, especially the passage from the *Zohar*, can be understood in this way. When our discussion is complete, the differences between this understanding and our presentation will be greatly minimized.

4. Israel, d. 1593.
5. Lithuania, d. 1893.
6. The Netziv provides another biblical episode that features the restrictive approach.

   To explain more we should preface our discussion with that which appears in the holy *Zohar* in this section — that Reuben said to throw Joseph into the pit filled with snakes and scorpions, and he did not fear that they would kill him because he relied on [Joseph's] merits. That which he did fear from the brothers [if he gave Joseph into their hands]

The full text of the *Zohar* reads (Genesis 185a–185b):

Rabbi Isaac said: If there were snakes and scorpions in [the pit], why does it say regarding Reuben, "In order to save him from their hands, to return him to his father." Was Reuben not concern with the fact that there were snakes and scorpions that could harm [Joseph]? How did he say [that his intentions were] "to return him to his father" and [how can the Torah claim that Reuben acted] "in order to save him?"

[The answer is:] Reuben saw that harm was possible in the hands of the brothers, for he knew how much they hated him, and that they desired to kill him. Reuben said: It is better for him to fall into a pit of snakes and scorpions [than to be] given over to the hands of his enemies who will have no mercy on him...

Here, in a place of snakes and scorpions, if he is righteous God will perform a miracle [and protect him], and at times the merit of one's forefathers can assist a person and save him. However, when he is given over to the hands of his enemy, there are few [individuals] who can be saved [from such a scenario]. For this reason Reuben said: "In order to save him from their hands." [Meaning:] from their hands specifically. And the [Torah did not just state]: "In order to save him," and no more.[7]

---

was because man's free will is above the realm of divine providence. I have an explicit proof to this, for it says in [the book of] Daniel, [chapter] six, when Cyrus threw [Daniel] into the lion's den, "And the king sealed it with his own signet...(in order) that nothing might be changed concerning Daniel" (Daniel 6:18). Meaning, he was sure that the lions wouldn't touch [Daniel] because they are not free-willed creatures; however, he was afraid lest he change his mind about Daniel [and arrange for a different method of punishment that would endanger Daniel].

7. In *Mareh Kohen*, the Talmud commentary of Rabbi Bezalel ben Moshe ha-Kohen of Vilna (Lithuania, d. 1878) to tractate *Shabbos* (22a), Rabbi Bezalel quotes the *Zohar* to answer the following question posed by Rabbi Shmuel Eliezer ben Yehudah Edels (Poland, d. 1631), the Maharsha, in his *Chidushei Agados* (*Chagigah*, chapter 1) in the name of Rabbi Eliyahu Mizrahi (Turkey, d. 1526): How did Reuben think he would be saving

The restrictive approach is also suggested by various Jewish thinkers in their analysis of King David's plea to God, immortalized in the daily *Tachanun* prayer (originally from Samuel II 24:10–14): "Let us fall into the hand of God, for His mercies are great, but let me not fall into human hands."

David angered God by ordering a national census, and after realizing his sin, pleaded with God to forgive him. God informed him that one of three possible punishments would befall him and the nation: enemy warfare, pestilence, or famine. David, with the above statement, emphatically chose pestilence, the punishment farthest removed from human activity.[8]

The Malbim explains David's reasoning as follows:

David saw that punishment of famine was [through] natural means, and the punishment of warfare was [through] free-willed [individuals]. Therefore, he chose the thing that was providential, for God's mercy is great.

• • •

There is also a tradition that the Rambam endorsed the restrictive approach. In the epistle of Rabbi Yosef Zundel of Salant, quoted in chapter 1, this tradition is recorded in the name of Rabbi Eliyahu of Vilna.

I heard from the pious one [i.e., the Gaon of Vilna], may his memory be blessed, and I as well have maintained since my youth, that there is an error which the masses believe — and even the Rambam concurs with this [erroneous] view — that a free-willed creature is able to affect an individual without a divine decree [to that effect].

Joseph by throwing him into the pit filled with snakes and scorpions, especially in light of the Talmud's statement in tractate *Yevamos* that if the courts have testimony regarding an individual stating that he fell into a pit containing scorpions, he is legally considered dead?

8. See *Rashi* on location why pestilence is considered less involved with human activity than famine.

Since the epistle does not cite a source within the Rambam's writings to substantiate this tradition, locating such a position within the Rambam's works is left to conjecture. One possible source is the Rambam's introduction to tractate *Avos*, entitled *Shemoneh Perakim*. In chapter 8 the Rambam affirms the principle of free will:

> When one robs another's money, or steals or cheats him, and [then] denies it and swears falsely regarding [his actions] — if we would [mistakenly] maintain that God decreed about this individual that he would receive this money, and [if we would maintain that God decreed] that [the money] would depart from the hand of the [victim], then [God would be] decreeing sin, and such is not the case. Rather all actions of man are given over to him, and dependent on his choices.

This source, however, does not necessarily represent the restrictive approach. It is true that the Rambam states that in cases of robbery there is not necessarily a divine decree that the robber would steal and that the victim would lose money, and the perpetrator is still able to accomplish his theft. However, it can easily be argued that the Rambam's point is not that there is no decree at all that the victim would lose money. Rather the Rambam's real point is that there is no decree that this specific individual would steal the money, and hence his free will is affirmed.

Other possible sources in the Rambam's writings are scattered comments in the *Moreh Nevuchim*. In section 2, chapter 29, the Rambam addresses the language of the prophets. He explains that every seer relates his prophecy through a unique style, and that those who study the prophetic writings must familiarize themselves with the styles of the particular prophet they are studying. As an example, the Rambam notes:

> Also the prophets, in referring to the destruction of a person, of a nation, or of a country, describe it as the result of God's great anger and wrath, while the prosperity of a nation is the result of God's pleasure and satisfaction.

Some read into this statement that the Rambam is implying that even though the prophet utilizes a language that credits God as the cause for all that transpires, such language is just stylistic, and is not the true intention of the prophet. However, it would be difficult to align the Rambam with the restrictive camp solely based on this implied proof.

Another suggested source is in section 3, chapter 12, where the Rambam discusses the erroneous view of many philosophers who maintain that the world is filled with more evil than goodness, more disappointment than joy. As part of his argument, the Rambam writes:

> Most of the evils that occur to a person are from him himself. That is, due to his own human shortcomings. It is the results of our own faults that we complain about and seek relief from. We suffer from the evils that we, by our own free will, inflict upon ourselves. Yet, we ascribe them to God. Heaven forbid! He is not connected with them!

The context of this statement, however, dispels the cogency of utilizing this source. The Rambam is dealing with individuals who chose to live base lives devoid of spirituality. They who merely pursue material pleasure are always disappointed, the Rambam argues. For instance, if one only seeks the most expensive, exquisite foods, then one will be miserable when fed average food. The Rambam argues that this misery is brought upon the person by his own bad choices, and is not the fault of God, nor a proof that the world is filled with disappointment and depression.

In sum, a cogent source for the Rambam's acceptance of the restrictive approach is still wanting. Moreover, the Rambam dedicates three chapters in *Moreh Nevuchim* to an in-depth discussion of divine providence, and nowhere is the restrictive approach mentioned. His silence in this section also leaves the issue, at best, unresolved.

There are those who claim that the Ramban, too, endorses the restrictive view. One such claim is made by Rabbi Avraham Shmuel

Binyamin Sofer[9] in his *Teshuvos Ketav Sofer* (*Orach Chayim* 136). Rabbi Sofer addresses the above-discussed event of Joseph's abandonment into the pit:

> And the Ramban writes that even though [in the pit Joseph] was in danger of being bitten by snakes and scorpions, and [in danger from] the water in [the pit], nonetheless [Reuben] decided it was better that [Joseph] should be in a pit of snakes, scorpions, and water, than to fall into the hands of men, who are free-willed creatures.

However, this supposed comment by the Ramban is not found in the extant versions of the Ramban's Torah commentary, as noted by Rabbi Ovadia Yosef in his *Teshuvos Yabiah Omer* (vol. 6, *Choshen Mishpat* 4:5). In fact, the Ramban's Torah commentary provides a completely different explanation of Reuben's attempt to save Joseph. Ramban suggests that Reuben was unaware of the fact the there were snakes and scorpions in the pit. He posits that the snakes and scorpions were hiding in cracks within the pit, or that the depth of the pit concealed them, and thus Reuben was unaware of their presence.[10] Not only does the Ramban fail to record the view of the *Zohar*, but he even provides a different explanation altogether.[11]

Another source in the Ramban that may have led people to believe that he endorses the restrictive approach is the Ramban's comments in Genesis 15:14, discussed in chapter 2, where he explains the culpability of the Egyptians as stemming from their persecuting the Israelites beyond the bounds of the divine decree. The implication of such a statement is that the divine decree only extended so

---

9.   Austria, 1871.

10. Rabbi Yom Tov ben Alisbili, the Ritva, also suggests this explanation in his commentary on *Shabbos* 22a.

11. The Maharsha also opts to not record the approach of the *Zohar*, perhaps an indication that he rejects the restrictive approach, as he explains (*Chagigah* 3a) that Reuben's intentions were to save Joseph because he said to throw Joseph into a pit that did not contain snakes or scorpions, and they instead threw him into a pit that did contain snakes and scorpions.

far, and when the Egyptians, as free-willed creatures, continued and intensified their persecution of the Israelites, this was against the divine decree — but nonetheless successfully realized. However, in chapter 2 we already developed an alternative explanation for the Ramban's statement,[12] and hence, this source is not necessarily indicative that the Ramban endorses the restrictive approach.

• • •

In closing this chapter, a caveat is in order: Even though the restrictive approach grants an individual possessing free will the ability to act and impact the lives of others without a divine decree, God clearly has the ability, and retains the prerogative, to intercede and foil the intended plans of any individual.

The Netziv states this caveat explicitly in a later passage in his above-quoted *Harchev Davar* (Genesis 37:21):

Heaven forbid we should say that God's providence is unable to protect someone, even from the free-willed decision of another individual. Rather we must say that [in order to be saved from another individual] much merit is required, in that he must be good even in issues between himself and his fellow, and he must be a righteous person who is afforded a good life on account of his being a completely righteous person.

---

12. In chapter 2 we wrote:

The Ra'avad and the Ramban are of the opinion that the Egyptians specifically were divinely decreed to be the vessels through which the Israelites would be enslaved; however, that enslavement had specific parameters and limits. This does not mean that the Israelites were not deserving of, or destined for, additional suffering. Indeed they were. But this additional suffering was not included within the parameters of the enslavement that the Egyptians were decreed to actualize. When the Egyptians stepped beyond the bounds of their divinely decreed role, and dealt exceedingly harshly with the Israelites, their actions were effective only because there was also a divine decree for this additional suffering.

CHAPTER 4
BRIDGING THE GAP

We have seen that there are two distinct approaches to assessing the ability of an individual possessing free will to impact others. The *traditional approach* argues that nothing occurs without a specific divine decree, and even the actions of an individual possessing free will are powerless if not divinely decreed. The more *restrictive approach* argues that only the actions of creatures devoid of free will are completely governed by divine decrees, while the actions of an individual possessing free will can impact others even without a divine decree.

While it is very likely that these views reflect divergent perspectives of man's ability and role in the world, in this chapter we will suggest that there is much commonality between these seemingly distinct approaches. Moreover, we will present philosophic constructs that suggest the possibility that there is no disagreement between the traditional approach and the restrictive approach.[1]

---

1. There are some seemingly contradictory statements made by Jewish thinkers that would indicate a commonality between the two approaches.

Note: The following discussions contain novel elements of thought that do not conform to our intuitive perceptions of reality. Patience and an open mind are advised in studying the remainder of this book.

Stage I:
Dangerous Situations

Our Sages were very concerned about people placing themselves in dangerous situations. The Talmud in *Ta'anis* (20b) charges: "It is prohibited for a man to walk under a dilapidated wall." In tractate *Bava Kama* (60a): "Once the angel of death is granted permission [to harm] he doesn't distinguish between the righteous and the evil." And in the Jerusalem Talmud (*Shabbos* 2): "Satan indicts [an individual] when he is in a dangerous situation."

These vexing statements are stated in reference to different forms of calamity. For example, the statement in *Bava Kama* warns an individual to be careful and health conscious during a plague.

But since a plague is not a free-willed creature, its effect on an individual, even according to those Jewish thinkers who espouse the restrictive approach, should be completely under the governance of divine providence. The plague's ability to harm an individual should simply be a function of whether a divine decree was issued against this particular individual. How can the Talmud suggest the contrary by warning an individual to be careful? The Talmud's enigmatic answer is that a situation that is likely to harm an individual (*shechiach hezeika*) is different.

So even in relation to objects that do not possess free will, there is seemingly a reality that a person can be harmed without a specific divine decree. This reality of *shechiach hezeika* is accepted even by those thinkers who endorse the traditional approach.

It should be obvious to the reader that the following discussion is not the only possible resolution to the issue and merely reflects one perspective.

STAGE II:
"PERMISSION" TO ACT

The Gaon of Vilna posits that there are two forms of providential issuances. The first is a formal decree that dictates a specific course of events. The second is an open-ended type of a decree that can best be classified as "permission." When this second form of decree is operating, worldly forces are granted dominion to act without a predetermined order. This creates a quasi state of havoc, as the force granted free reign is unleashed in the world. If man is directly threatened by such a force, the only way for him to be spared is if God actively intercedes and saves him. The Gaon's position is recorded in *Sefer Imrei Noam, Berachos* (33b):

> When an animal attacks it is on account of two [possible] reasons. The first is that such was the [direct] decree [of God] against this man, as it is stated, "If a snake bites without being charmed" (Ecclesiastes 10:11). [The Midrash explains: "The snake doesn't bite unless it is charmed from Heaven."] The second reason is if [the animal] is sent out (*mushlach*).
>
> The difference [between these two reasons] is if it is decreed upon a person, so then [it only affects] the subject of the decree, based on sin. But, when the animal is *mushlach* it doesn't distinguish between good [people] and evil [people], and it harms whomever it encounters.

Animals and objects that do not possess free will can operate in either of the above functions. In general they are bound by direct decrees, and hence can only harm an individual if an explicit decree to that effect was issued by God. However, in certain situations these creatures are *mushlach*, granted "permission" to act without a predetermined course of action.

This second classification is similar to the concept of *shechiach hezeika*. If an individual is situated in a place or scenario that is classified as *shechiach hezeika*, he can be harmed even without a specific decree against him. In order to be saved from such a fate he would require increased merits for divine intercession on his behalf.[2]

Rabbi Bachya ibn Paquda was quoted in the beginning of chapter 1 as declaring: "No creation has the ability to bring benefit or harm to himself or another without the acquiescence of God." But Rabbi Bachya, and all the Jewish thinkers in the traditional camp, are forced to agree that this second, open-ended form of a divine decree is also considered "the acquiescence of God," just as they must accept the reality of *shechiach hezeika*.

The concepts of "permission" and *shechiach hezeika* can be used to understand the actions of a human being endowed with free will. We can suggest that all actions of a human being are classified as, or at least similar to, a scenario of *shechiach hezeika*. In other words, God grants man "permission," or free reign, to act as he pleases, similar to the way He grants a disease free reign during a plague. With this "permission" he can harm another individual even without the issuance of a specific decree. Yet still, the result of this ability does not lie outside the purview of "the acquiescence of God."

Our suggestion to classify all human activity in a similar category with *shechiach hezeika* finds precedence in tractate *Pesachim* (8a). The Talmud states that a person is not required to search before Passover for leavened products under a pile of fallen stones, for such a search could be dangerous due to the presence of scorpions. The Talmud questions this leniency from the principle that "one involved in the performance of a commandment is not harmed." The Talmud responds that "a situation of *shechiach hezeika* is different" and in such a scenario the individual performing the commandment is not afforded the protection normally granted. As a proof text that even one performing a commandment is not afforded divine protection when the case is considered *shechiach hezeika*, the Talmud quotes a verse from Samuel I (16:2) that records Samuel's

2. This understanding sheds light on the Talmudic dictum in tractate *Shabbos* (32): "Man should never stand in a dangerous situation and say that a miracle will occur on his behalf, for perhaps a miracle will not occur, and if a miracle does occur it subtracts merits from him."

reservations about locating and anointing a new king (David), during the reign of Saul. "And Samuel said: 'How can I go? If Saul hears it, he will kill me.' And God said: 'Take a heifer with you.' "

The Talmud's quotation of Samuel's concern that Saul would harm him as a proof text for the notion of *shechiach hezeika* indicates that the free will of an individual, and its possible ill effects on another, is classified as *shechiach hezeika*.

And so we see that when Jewish thinkers asserting the restrictive approach claim that an individual endowed with free will can impact others without a divine decree, the Jewish thinkers of the traditional camp can, in theory, agree with such an assertion, for they too admit that in certain cases, such as a case of *shechiach hezeika* (or we can refer to it as *mushlach* according to the Vilna Gaon's presentation), an individual can be affected without a direct divine decree.

STAGE III:
NATURAL ORDER VS. SUPERNATURAL ORDER

Although we have demonstrated theoretical commonality between the traditional approach and the restrictive approach, in that both admit to situations where events occur without a specific divine decree,[3] further understanding is required to bridge the two camps. But first, we must address an internal perplexity that presents itself within the traditional approach.

How can the Jewish thinkers who endorse the traditional approach, and assert that everything that occurs to an individual is the direct result of a divine decree, also accept the second form of provi-

---

3.   That is, for those endorsing the restrictive approach: all situations involving individuals endowed with free will and situations involving non-free-willed creatures when it is *shechiach hezeika* (or the Gaon of Vilna's *mushlach*). For those endorsing the traditional approach — only situations involving non-free-willed creatures when it is *shechiach hezeika* (or the Gaon of Vilna's *mushlach*).

dential issuances that reign in situations of *shechiach hezeika*? When "permission" is granted to a force, and a quasi state of havoc ensues, the resultant impact on individuals is seemingly not the "direct result of a divine decree." How can these thinkers fully maintain that everything is completely divinely ordained, and at the same time accept the second form of providential issuances? In other words: Granted we have proven that they do accept the concept of *shechiach hezeika*, but how is this acceptance tenable in light of their general understanding of divine providence?

To scratch the surface of the issue, we must re-explore God's providential relationship with the world. We developed in Part One of this book the concurrent systems of *hanhagas ha-mishpat* and *hanhagas ha-yichud*. *Hanhagas ha-mishpat* is the system of reward and punishment, where man is rewarded for his proper behavior and punished for his sins. However there is an additional system operating in the world. All that exists in the world was created with the eventual goal of manifesting the glory of God in the world: "All was created for His glory" (*Avos* 6:11) This goal finds expression in the end of days when all people and creations will declare the glory of God. *Hanhagas ha-yichud* is the ever-unfolding process of the eventual divine manifestation. All creations and history are part of an evolutionary process that is building toward a revelation of God's glory, and this process operates concurrently in our world with the system of reward and punishment.

Similar to the dichotomy of *hanhagas ha-yichud* and *hanhagas ha-mishpat*, there are two other providential systems that operate concurrently.

Before we outline these systems we must stress that God's governance of the world is infinitely more complex than we can ever grasp, and certainly express. Our goal is to shed light on a topic we will never understand, for we, constricted by human limitations, are attempting to fathom something outside the realm of humanity. In addition to this disclaimer, we must also humbly realize that in truth there are no formal barriers or classifications for God's dealings. We merely assign names and categories to God's doings as a human attempt to come to grips with the unfathomable. All titles and classifications discussed below are merely attempts to conceptualize, from a human vantage point, God's ways. It is with this goal in mind that we will now suggest another two-tiered system of God's providential influence in the world.

In the second introduction to *Gevuros Hashem*, the Maharal, Rabbi Yehudah Loew ben Bezalel,[4] addresses the nature of miracles, and their impact on the world. He develops that the world contains two dimensions of reality, the natural order and the transcendental (or supernatural) order. Both dimensions exist and operate at the same time; however, generally humanity only perceives the natural order. In rare cases, God removes the veil and reveals the transcendental order. Hence, when God caused the sun to stop while Joshua and the Israelites waged war in Givon, the Maharal argues that the rest of the world continued in its normal course of existence.[5]

A miracle is not an anomaly or aberration in nature, rather the natural world always stays its course, and miracles transpire in a separate dimension, the transcendental order, which exists as an overlay to this world. While the transcendental order is normally unperceivable, in instances of miracles, such as when God caused the sun to stop, God reveals the transcendental order — the arena of the miraculous — and allows the participants of the miracle to experience life in the transcendental order. Therefore, the Maharal argues, only those involved in the battle actually perceived daylight on that fateful day in Givon; other bystanders were not privy to the miraculous daylight and were clouded in the natural darkness. In essence, there existed in Givon on that specific day in history both daylight and darkness at the same time.

To better grasp the strange reality we are suggesting — that two opposite realities can function simultaneously in the world — or in

---

4.   Prague, d. 1609.

5.   Maharal's expression is *"Olam ke-minhago noheg."*

other words, to better understand the concept of an indiscernible dimension that exists concomitantly with the natural order, consider the following:[6]

> Suppose there exists somewhere a race of flat people. Their world and universe consists of a point, a line, and even a two-dimensional plane surface, but no more. A three-dimensional body has no meaning to an inhabitant of this world. Let us further suppose that these beings develop laws of geometry, which they use locally and find to be perfectly valid.
>
> As time passes on, these people begin to broaden their horizons; they travel greater and greater distances. They discover, through experience, mysterious properties of their reality which seems to them to be of the utmost strangeness.
>
> Originally, a traveler who started out at point A and traveled to point B would reverse directions in order to return to his point of origin. After following this procedure for many years, a certain brave explorer makes a remarkable discovery: their flat world has the amazing property of repeating itself. That is, if a traveler begins at point A and travels to B, he may return to his origin by merely continuing in a straight line in the same direction [i.e., past point B]. Of course he may still use the original method for returning to his origin if he so wishes. However, he will no doubt often find it more expedient to continue in a straight line. After years and years of careful experimentation the navigators of this world firmly establish the fact that their world has the remarkable property of endlessly repeating itself.
>
> The story does not end here, but rather just begins. For there is another race of beings that had taken interest in our two-dimensional people. This race, however, experiences an added

---

6. This parable was written by Rabbi Shlomo Mallin and Dr. Zvi Faier and appears in footnote 9 of Rabbi Mallin's *Book of Divine Power* (New York: Feldheim Publishers, 1975). However, it appears that the basis of Rabbi Mallin's parable is from British author Edwin Abbott's *Flatland* (published in 1884).

dimension; they live in a three-dimensional world. They are not at all surprised that the flat people can return to their point of origin by continuing in the same direction in a straight line. Relative to them the flat world of these [flat] people is the surface of a cylinder...

Since the three-dimensional people perceive the curvature of a flat surface, as their perception includes a third dimension, they easily understand how point A can be reached by traveling beyond point B. For example, if point A is New York, and one travels in a line that extends across the Atlantic Ocean, across Europe, Asia, and the Pacific Ocean and ends at point B, which is in California, it is possible to return to New York in one of two ways. The first is to retrace the line backwards and re-cross the Pacific Ocean, travel back across Asia and Europe, and finally cross the Atlantic Ocean back to New York, or one can simply continue forward past California across the United States and arrive in New York, covering much less distance. For a three-dimensional person the second option is the obvious choice; but for a person who only experiences two dimensions, the world is flat, and the concept of continuing past California to reach New York is unfathomable.

At this stage it is important to emphasize that neither the view of the two- or three-dimensional beings is "wrong." Each race is entitled to its view, and indeed valid predictions, theoretical structures, and profound insight into reality can be obtained from either or both of these views...

The moral of the story is that there is not one, but many valid ways in which reality expresses its order. All of these aspects are basic and intrinsic facets of reality, and we are entitled to any one or many of the valid views we can relate to. Certain situations compel us to recognize a reality greater than the one we can grasp with our senses. We thus have a great deal in common with the two-dimensional people of this story.

The above story demonstrates how an individual trapped in a limited reality cannot fathom dimensions beyond his experiences.

Two-dimensional beings, whose world is but a plane, cannot understand why going beyond point B brings them back to point A. According to the scientific systems they developed, there is no way to account for this phenomenon.

But as an individual who perceives the third dimension can easily understand, following beyond point B to reach point A is very logical. Yet, no matter how hard the three-dimensional person tries, he is unable to explain to the two-dimensional individual the concept of a third dimension. Due to his limited perceptions, a two-dimensional being cannot possible grasp the third dimension. There is no "outward" for him; everything he has ever experienced is flat, including himself, and so he cannot begin to understand an outward direction.[7] The most the two-dimensional being can do is admit that another dimension exists, realizing he will never perceive it as it truly is. Traveling beyond point B back to point A helps him with this admission. Although he can't conceptualize how the third dimension operates, he can come to a realization that the third dimension indeed exists.

The point of our parabolic story is to underscore that *reality as we perceive it does not necessarily reflect the ultimate reality.* The possibility of an additional dimension to life, as the Maharal argues about the transcendental realm, is not only logically feasible, but actually quite likely. Certain events in our lives, or the history of our nation, force us to a realization that a transcendental (supernatural) realm exists, even though we do not understand how it is possible.

Stage IV:
Two Concurrent Realities

Rabbi Tzadok ha-Kohen of Lublin uses the concept that an additional transcendent dimension exists concurrently with the natural

---

7.   Indeed, if a hole was drilled through the cylinder from point A to point B, an even faster way to travel back from B to A would be achieved. The two-dimensional figures could embark on the journey, see that it is indeed faster, but still never grasp it conceptually.

order to explain a famous dispute regarding one of the Rambam's statements in *Mishneh Torah*. In *Hilchos Teshuvah* (5:5) the Rambam writes:

Perhaps one may say: Behold God knows everything that will occur before it transpires, He knows that this [individual] will be righteous or evil. Or, perhaps He does not know. If He knows that [this individual] will be a righteous person, it is impossible that he will not be a righteous person. And if you maintain that [God] knows he will be a righteous person, but it is [still] possible he will be an evil person, behold He does not know the facts completely.

You should know that the answer to this perplexity is "a measure longer than the earth, and broader than the sea" (Job 11:9), and many major principles and lofty mountains [i.e., esoteric concepts] are dependent upon it. However, you need to know and understand that which I am saying.

We already explained in the second chapter of *Hilchos Yesodei ha-Torah* that God's knowledge is not distinct from His being, as is the case by man: they and their knowledge are distinct. Rather He, God, and His knowledge are one. The human mind is unable to completely fathom this concept. For just as man is unable to completely fathom and grasp the truth [i.e., existence] of God, as the verse states, "For man will not see Me, and live" (Exodus 33:20), so, too, man is unable to fathom and grasp the knowledge of God. This is the intention of the prophet, "For My thoughts are not your thoughts, neither are your ways My ways" (Isaiah 55:8). And since this is true, we do not possess the power to know how God knows all of the creations and their doings.

However, we do know without a doubt that man's actions are in his own hands. God does not pull him [in one direction], nor does He decree upon him not to do this or not to do that. We do not know this based on blind faith alone, but rather [we know this] based on clear philosophical proofs.

The Ra'avad's understanding of the Rambam's statement is that mortal man cannot understand the paradoxical existence of God's foreknowledge and man's free will, and hence the solution eludes mankind. For this approach, the Ra'avad censures the Rambam:

> This author [i.e., the Rambam] did not act wisely, for a person should not start something if he is unable to finish it. He began with questions and problems and left the issue unresolved, and in the end relied upon faith. It would have been better for him to leave the issue simply [i.e., without raising the question] of the unsophisticated, and not to rile up their minds [just to] leave them in doubt, [for now] perhaps they will, for one moment, think unsettling thoughts regarding this.

To salvage the situation, the Ra'avad then suggests a possible solution to this paradox, but records his reservations:

> Even though there isn't a fully satisfactory answer to this, it will be good for [the Rambam] if I assist him with a partial solution. If the righteousness and villainy of an individual were dependent on a divine decree, we would [be forced] to conclude that His knowledge is [synonymous with] his decree,[8] and then this paradox would be very challenging; however, now that God has removed this control [i.e., the power to actively orchestrate everything] and placed it in the hands of man himself, [God's] knowledge is no longer [synonymous with] His decree. Rather [God's knowledge is now comparable to] the knowledge of astrologers, who know through other forces what will be the future of an individual...this type of knowledge is not the same as a decree. However, this whole [answer] does not suffice.

Rabbi Tzadok disagrees with the critique of the Ra'avad.[9] Us-

---

8.   If God's knowledge is synonymous with His decree, then the fact God knows something is the same as if he decrees it to be. Accordingly God's knowledge would force things to occur.

9.   Many later readers of this passage in *Mishneh Torah* also argue with the Ra'avad's critique. They suggest that the Rambam was providing a solution. According to them, the Rambam argues that just as God is not bound by space and can exist at all places at the same time, so too God is not bound

ing the above-developed concept that an additional transcendent dimension exists concurrently with the natural order, Rabbi Tzadok argues that the Rambam most certainly provided a resolution to the paradox of free will and divine foreknowledge.[10] The resolution is that both fully exist. In the natural world man is granted free will, and possesses the ability to act as he so desires — we can refer to this as the *olam ha-bechirah* (the world of free will). However, there is an additional dimension that exists, like the Maharal's supernatural realm, not perceivable by the human eye. In this transcendent reality, which we can will call the *olam ha-yediah* (the world of foreknowledge), God's knowledge and decrees are in complete control.[11] Granted it is impossible for man to conceptualize how both of these worlds can co-exist,[12] but such a limitation of human perception

---

by time and can therefore exist at all points of history at the same time. His knowledge of the future therefore does not translate into a decree and force such events to occur (which is the case of man's time-bound knowledge). This leaves room for man's free will.

Rabbi Yitzchak Izik Chaver (Wildmann) (Lithuania, d. 1853) might be understanding the Rambam this way in *Siach Yitzchak* (vol. 2, *likutim* 2): "For God's knowledge is not like our knowledge — which is divided into past years and future years..." Ironically, some suggest that this "time" approach is the Ra'avad's solution.

10. An antinomy is a dialectic illusion in which two contradictory theses both appear rationally correct. Rabbi Tzadok seeks to resolve the antinomy by demonstrating that what is proven involves a failure to appreciate the limits of possible experience.

11. This appears to be his intent in *Pri Tzadik, Bamidbar*, p. 98, and *Devarim*, pp. 89 and 196. Rabbi Tzadok quotes this approach in the names of *Zohar ha-Chadash* and Rabbi Yitzchak ben Shlomo Luria (Egypt-Israel, d. 1572), the Ari z"l, in his *sefer Arba Meos Shekel Kesef*. See also Rabbi Tzadok's *Takanas ha-Shavim*, chapter 6, for an expansive discussion and exposition of this approach.

12. Just as it is impossible for man to conceptualize how darkness and daylight existed concurrently in Givon during Joshua's battle. Rabbi Tzadok declares (*Sefer ha-Zichronos, Mitzvah* 3 and *Pri Tzadik, Yisro* #3): "Where there is divine knowledge, there is no free will. And where there is free will, there is no divine knowledge." Or, in other words, in the *olam ha-yediah* there is no free will and in the *olam ha-bechirah* there is no foreknowledge.

does not exclude the veracity of their concurrent existence.

For the sake of sharpening our understanding: We could have suggested that really there is only one reality — that everything is decreed by God, and free will is merely a mirage, a function of man's perception and man's inability to grasp the true reality.[13] However, we are not suggesting this. We are suggesting that there are actually two distinct realities that exist concurrently. Man's perception of free will is the truth, in one dimension; but simultaneously another dimension exists where free will is not the operative force, and where divine decrees reign supreme.

STAGE V: RESOLVING THE PARADOX

With the above-developed concepts we can shed light on the internal perplexity noted in those who endorse the traditional approach.[14] In the natural world, animals and other creatures are

---

13. On a superficial level it appears that Rabbi Mordechai Yosef Leiner presents an understanding like this in his Torah commentary *Mei ha-Shiloach* (*Vayera*), ascribing our perception of free will as a mirage.

    This concept is very deep. That which appears in the Talmud, "All is in the hands of Heaven except for the fear of Heaven" is only according to the limits of man's intellectual ability to perceive reality. However, in truth everything is in the hands of Heaven, even the fear of Heaven — it is only in this world that God masks His ways.

    However, in light of our discussion here, we can begin to understand Rabbi Leiner's true intentions.

14. We asked above: How can the Jewish thinkers who endorse the traditional approach, and assert that everything that occurs to an individual is the direct result of a divine decree, also accept the second form of providential issuances that reign in situations of *shechiach hezeika*. When "permission" is granted to a force, and a quasi state of havoc ensues, the resultant impact on individuals is seemingly not the "direct result of a divine decree." How can these thinkers fully maintain that everything is completely divinely ordained, and at the same time accept the second form of providential issuances?

granted "permission" to reign freely. Similarly, dangerous situations, such as a dilapidated wall, follow a natural course (from the perspective of the natural world). And so, when the dilapidated wall is hit by a falling tree branch, the wall falls and may even kill a negligent individual standing beside it. However the fact that the forces of *shechiach hezeika* exist in the natural world does not preclude the possibility that in the transcendental realm the dilapidated wall falling and killing an individual fulfills a divine decree.

In the transcendental dimension, everything is ordained and operates based on divine decrees. At the depths of reality, God oversees all that transpires. People are impacted *within the natural order* without a specific decree; however, in the the transcendental dimension, there was certainly a divine decree. While conception of this coexistence is impossible,[15] realization of its existence is possible.

It is important to stress: Man is forced to live in the natural world and operate in the *olam ha-bechirah*; he must therefore abide by the rules of that dimension. Accordingly, he is held accountable for the results of his free will, and is charged with a responsibility, as the Talmudic statements above demand, to protect himself from dangerous situations.

Stage VI: The Bridge — A Question of Perspective

This enigma of reality also serves to bridge the traditional approach and the restrictive approach. The restrictive approach is true regarding the natural dimension — an individual possessing free will has the ability to harm an individual without the presence of a divine decree. This is the perspective man must have when engaging

---

15. Rabbi Tzadok explains that this was the Rambam's intent when he quoted, "For My thoughts are not your thoughts, neither are your ways My ways" (Isaiah 55:8).

the world.[16]

It is for this reason that in every instance the restrictive approach is documented it addresses a specific human scenario. For instance, what is better for Joseph — to be in the hands of the brothers or in the pit filled with snakes and scorpions? Or what is better for David and his people — to be in the hands of their enemies or the victims of a plague? For the proper response to natural world situations, Jewish thinkers invoke the restrictive approach.

However, this does not mean that these same thinkers do not admit that in the transcendental realm — or shall we say, from God's perspective — everything is divinely decreed. Ultimately, the fate of Joseph was no doubt the product of a divine decree, and not the mere result of the brother's free will. When one is interested less in how man should react, and more in search of the ultimate cause behind events, the focus turns to the divine decree.

Indeed, the Ohr ha-Chayim himself, the cardinal proponent of the restrictive approach, states this explicitly in his commentary on Genesis (45:8):

> Now, after [Joseph] saw everything that evolved from his descent to Egypt, his knew that the entire ordeal was from God, and that [the brothers] were fulfilling His mission and it was not their own doings. And on account of this there is no reason to harbor hatred, nor to deny them brotherly feelings.

---

16. This is similar to the fact that a man has free will to act in this world, even though God has foreknowledge of all that will transpire. In a sense, the differing views in our discussion are the two sides of the issue of free will versus divine foreknowledge discussed in the *Rambam, Hilchos Teshuvah*. The restrictive approach merely stresses the free will side of the issue, for man must exist in the world with the realization of his free will. However, after one is wronged, the author of the *Sefer ha-Chinuch* suggests stressing the other side of the issue and realizing that what was perpetrated was also decreed by God.

EPILOGUE

Understanding that all of creation is graced with God's personal attention certainly deepens an individual's intellectual grasp of reality. But the challenge still exists to perceive that Godly interaction in daily life. With the information presented in the above chapters, man is challenged to live life on a higher plateau. It is not enough to understand; rather, the reader is called upon to internalize. Experiencing God's presence in all areas of life, even during the most mundane exercises, is a religious imperative.

Religious life has many built-in techniques for constant realization of divine providence. Daily life is teeming with opportunities to perform Torah commandments. It is up to man to use these opportunities to bolster perception of the divine.

For example, a mezuzah attached to the doorpost of every room allows an individual to remember God at the crucial moment before entering. Interaction with the mezuzah should not be restricted to a mere kiss, but the more important interaction is the reminding oneself of God's presence in the room. Before entering the room for a business deal, or to ask a parent for a favor, the internalization of the mezuzah allows one to remember that God's active participation is necessary for success.

Even the most mundane behavior, such as a trip to the bathroom, can be transformed into a religious experience. While the blessing of *Asher Yatzar* is classically understood to be a statement of thanks to God for the miracle of the human body, Rabbi Mayer Twersky notes an alternative perspective. Based on a comment of the *Chovos ha-Levavos*, Rabbi Twersky suggests that an additional intent of *Asher Yatzar* is to thank God for the frailty of the human body. God created man in such a way that human vulnerability is a tangible reality. We see often how the smallest deviation from normal functioning can have painful, and even life threatening, ramifications. The reality of human vulnerability forces man to constantly remember the human need for divine providence in even the most mundane areas of life.

"God is your protection [lit. shadow or shade] upon your right hand" (Psalms 121). The *Nefesh ha-Chayim* of Rabbi Chayim Volozhiner[1] (1:7) explains this verse metaphorically, that God is akin to man's shadow. He responds to our movements. The more we live with a realization of His presence, the more God allows His presence to be perceived.

May our newfound understanding of God's governance encourage us to live, and God to shower, our lives with a heightened sense of divine consciousness.

---

1.   Lithuania, d. 1821.

In loving memory of
our husband and father

Leon Leibowitz

אריה לייב בן סנדר אשר ז״ל

Beloved and most pleasant in life

May his memory be a blessing

ת.נ.צ.ב.ה.

Dedicated by the Leibowitz Family

In loving memory of
our husband and father

Ruby Perchick

ראובן בן יעקב הלוי ז״ל

Who taught us the values
we try to live by

May his memory be a blessing

ת.נ.צ.ב.ה.

Dedicated by the Perchick Family

Made in the USA
Las Vegas, NV
04 September 2022

54704431R00095